A LIVING LEGACY

Memories from the Past with a Message for Today

By Charles Vandegriffe

Missouri Center for the Book

Missouri Authors Collection

Acknowledgments

Putting this book together has been such a wonderful journey. So many people have come together to help me realize this dream. It hardly seems possible to thank everyone, and words cannot adequately express my appreciation.

I want to thank the North County Journal, part of Pulitzer Inc.'s Suburban Journals of Greater St. Louis. They were the first to provide me with the opportunity to share my memories with the readers in the community.

I want to thank the many organizations that have invited me to speak. Sharing with them memories of an era gone by has helped to generate more memories.

It is with much gratitude that I acknowledge B. Kay Coulter, my co-writer and editor. Without her organizational and editing skills, this book would have not come into being. Her previously published works are *Proverbs for Personalities* (Goss Publishing 2000), *Victim/Victor: It's Your Choice* (Xulon Press 2002) and *Free to Be* (Xulon Press 2004) and she has been a featured author at the International Christian Booksellers Convention since 2002.

I especially want to thank my wife, Betty, who has been my steadfast supporter, lifelong friend and soul mate. She is truly the love of my life, and she deserves more thanks than I can possibly give for all the support she has given me through it all.

For the rest of my family, especially Chuck, Cathie, Mark and Kevin and my many friends that I have accumulated through the years—you have helped make my life so complete. Without you, I wouldn't have so many wonderful memories to share, and the journey wouldn't have been nearly as sweet.

But most of all, I want to thank God for blessing me with so many wonderful gifts in my life and for giving me the ability to remember life as it was, relative to the society of the 30s, 40s and 50s. He has made my life truly rich, and for that I am eternally grateful.

Foreword

My father asked me a simple yet overwhelming question about the book he was in the process of writing. Do you think that people want to hear my story? Being the oldest of four children, I felt a great responsibility to answer my father in the most honest and sincere way. I said yes. "No, no," he said, "really…this story I feel so compelled to write, is it interesting enough to move people to remember their stories of life and in turn share them with others? Is it meaningful enough to move a mature person who believes they no longer are needed? What about those who think that they don't have anything to share? Will the messages concerning the decline in morality, honesty and all the other traditional values be enough to move young people to search the past for answers? To search the counsel of elders in their own families—great grandparents, grandparents and parents? Inspire them to take the best from the past and apply it to their lives? Oh, to reach the fire in the heart and soul of people! To make them understand that each human being has a chance to touch another life in meaningful ways just by reaching out. I think this book can inform, enlighten and move people to action."

Dad, I think you have answered your own question. I and anybody I know seeks to improve their lives and the lives of the ones they love. But, we all get lost in the words to some degree and need a beacon to draw us back on course. This book could be one of these guides—a symbol of what was and is, to some degree, right with the world. It is a "how to" on ensuring a happy and constructive life which contributes to everyone's success.

Dad replied, "But I have a problem. What is it? Well, between every word, sentence and page, other words come into my mind—so many that if I were to write them all down, the book would never end. This is one of those life lessons to me. What's that? That no matter how hard one tries in life to do something perfectly, we always leave something out. I hope the readers of this book fill in the gaps with their own life's experiences. If they then will pass them on to just one person, just one—to take from a beautiful song— "What a wonderful world this would be!"

Charles H. Vandegriffe Jr.

Contents

Introduction

The world is changing at what seems like a breath-taking speed. We rush headlong into the future, not taking time to glean from the past those things which make our nation and way of life strong. In this process we need to stop and ask, "What is the legacy we leave our children?" If not we who are senior citizens, then who will teach them the values and strength of character that is still needed in society? Who will model for them morality, integrity, and respect for authority?

This book explores the memory banks of many alive today who experienced crisis times in our nation like The Great Depression, World War II, the bombing of Pearl Harbor, the decline of morals, and the change from an industrial society to a technological one. We have seen and are seeing current days of crisis as well, from the bombing of the World Trade Centers in September 2001 to the continuing War on Terrorism. I believe our society should learn from our senior citizens their perspective on current events in light of history. Seniors have much to say and have wisdom to offer if anybody wants to listen.

This book not only deals with very serious matters but also takes a look into the past to remember better times, simpler times, and pleasurable times. There are times when we long for the "good ole' days." All this change going on is disturbing and we are at times unsure of ourselves and how we fit into a society that often ignores the council of the elderly.

A Living Legacy is based on 150 articles which I wrote from 2001-2004 for the "North County Journals," a part of Pulitzer Inc.

"Suburban Journals of Greater St. Louis." The sources for much of the memories recounted herein come from older people whom I have had the pleasure of meeting as I traveled the country in speaking engagements. I would recommend even to our politicians that they do the same thing—not just talking but rather listening to what we have to say. Perhaps in this way (if they heed our advice) they would be in a better position to lead our nation with high standards of morality, integrity, and character.

It is my sincere hope that you, the reader, enjoys this walk down "memory lane," and that you will be encouraged to speak out, even if it is with your own children and grandchildren. This is part of the legacy we leave, and it is invaluable.

1930-1939
"Years of Struggle"

Unemployment and poverty characterized the 1930s in this country, dominating the lives of many. Franklin Roosevelt was elected president in 1932, offering a "new deal" for Americans through a wide-ranging recovery program. Dust storms in the Midwestern states starting in 1933 forced many farmers to abandon their lands and move on. In Europe, political turmoil led to the rise of the extremely nationalist and racist Nazi Party in Germany. The end of the decade saw the onset of the second World War within 25 years. There were some bright spots in the news, however—like the building of the Empire State Building which put an army of laborers to work; the opening of a nationwide bus service provided by the Greyhound Company; the offering of federal aid to the Dust Bowl states; and the forming of a national farm policy.

For the survivors of the traumatic thirties the stage was set for better times to come. The traumatic events shaped the character of those who lived through this decade. Much can be learned by listening to their stories.

SECTION 1

FAMILY HEIRLOOMS

CHAPTER ONE

Family

In modern-day America, there currently is a controversial matter concerning what the word "family" means. For those of us of the older generation (born in the '30s, '40s, and '50s of the twentieth century) we have no need of a new definition for family. We know what it is and what it means to the continuation of our nation. The family is the bedrock of our nation. There is an old saying that goes like this: "As the family goes, so goes the nation." [11]

We as senior citizens are very concerned about where our nation is going. We do not like what we see and we long for things to be as they were in the "good ole' days." In this section of the book we are going to take a snapshot approach to just what those "good ole' days" meant for families. We will cover everything from parental responsibilities to the just plain fun stuff of children in that day and age. If the reader is one born after the sixties, you are going to need to use your imagination. For the rest of you, I want to just jar your memories of happier times.

Let's fantasize for awhile. Do you sometimes want to resign from being an adult and return to the age of ten? Well, let's see where your imagination takes you. Remember going to the local café (in my case it was the Parkmor or White Castle) and you thought you were dining in a fancy restaurant? You were not worrying about your sugar level or your cholesterol. No way were you going to have a diet soda—I don't even remember if they had a diet drink back then, but you see my point. You were more likely to order a

chocolate malt and since you are fantasizing (which is calorie-free), you would tell them to make it extra thick so that you couldn't suck it through a straw.

Wouldn't it be nice to have a mindset that everyone in the world is honest, good and trustworthy? This would make you unmindful of the tragedies of life and you would be able to experience joy to the fullest, even in little things. Your day's agenda would consist of things like washing your bike and attaching some new cards for the spokes to hit to make that imaginary motor sound. Contrast this to today's responsibilities and worries like your computer crashing or losing your cell phone, not to mention losing your 401k in the Stock Market.

Let's get back to those childhood memories. How about having dreams about being a ball player for the Cardinals baseball team or being the leading lady in a movie, and being uninhibited in giving smiles and hugs. You would really believe that dreams come true and would have these dreams as you lay on the grass looking up at the blue sky while billowing clouds roll by.

* * * * *

Historical Moment from 1939
Long-awaited Hollywood premier of "Gone With the Wind."
Starring Clark Gable and Vivien Leigh, this Civil War epic
is certain to be a box-office hit.

* * * * *

Now, are you ready to say that you will turn in your computer, cell phone, savings account, mortgage payment books, and all of your entertainment centers and officially resign from being an adult? Not me! As far as I am concerned, I do not want to resign from adulthood. Being ten years old was great at the time and so was each stage of life following, even with trials and hardships. I think that the Lord has given us the strength to endure the hardships at each point of life and has let us experience the joys we had as well. But that time has passed and we seniors are now at a wonderful time of life, even with the sufferings we have to endure at this stage. Some are blessed with good health with very little problems but others are not so blessed. In many ways though there are no more battles to fight, such as getting that promotion, going to night school to get that advanced education, hoping and praying the car will start in the morning so that you can get to work, etc.

Now is the time to share our knowledge, based on our experiences, with the younger generation and watch them learn and stumble, picking them up and seeing them mature into beautiful adults. We have learned many lessons along the way, and have the privilege and opportunity of teaching them the history of our nation from the wars, political scenes, floods, and Depression, as well as the good times. What fun we had in going to dances, having our dates, going to school and basically enjoying the simpler life. We also had a strong sense of values. A person's handshake was a contract, for example. Honesty and goodness were valued highly. So, take the good things of life that you had at age ten and cherish the memories, but realize too that you have much to pass on to those who will outlive you.

CHAPTER TWO

Growing Up

Dental Hygiene

I want to talk about the little things that make "growing up" so memorable. Did you ever notice, as we get older, we are always telling the younger generation about "then and now" relative to those very minute details that made growing up so very different from today? Let's take, for example, brushing your teeth. As a boy on the farm I was required to brush my teeth once a week with baking soda and salt. My dentist was my grandfather (the local blacksmith). He would take me to the shop, hold my head with his enormous hands and say, "Open wide." Fear struck my entire body as he pulled my baby teeth. We were not allowed to show fear, but I think I cheated, as I was fearful. Was it cruel? No, that is just the way it was in that day and time. Upon completion of the procedure, I washed my mouth out with salt water and thanked God that the ordeal was over. To this day I can still feel those snub-nosed pliers touching my front teeth as he went for the "target." However, in spite of the rather primitive technique of tooth extraction and dental hygiene (or lack thereof), I must say I have my own teeth today, and with the aid of my dentist I am supporting a modern day cap job covering up those original teeth that were maintained once a week with baking soda and salt. We have come a long way—many toothpaste companies are advertising that their products contain (would you believe it?) baking soda! How about that! I guess my grandmother knew what she was doing. It is interesting to note that even though we brushed our teeth only once a week, we did not have the cavities and dental problems in those days because we did not get much store-bought candy, either. Today, some sixty plus years later, I still have a majority of my teeth.

Homemade Goodies

Remember how on a Saturday evening we would make homemade ice cream? I have never tasted any modern day ice cream that would surpass that wonderful taste. Maybe it was the cool clean breeze of the evening and the wonderful loving family that surrounded the event that added to the taste of that "cream," as we affectionately called it. To keep our dairy products cold, we put them in a pail and lowered them down into a well, which also provided us drinking water. We had no filters or any devices to screen the water, but it was clean and cold and it tasted good and refreshing.

Canning time, as I remember it, was a great time of the year. Do you remember the Mason jars? We could not do without those jars. Making apple butter was a chore for the women and children. The women would peel the apples and put them in this big black cast iron belly pot and the children would use an enormous wooden paddle to continuously stir the apples as they cooked. I remember the invention of a spindle device that you stuck the apple on and with a handle you would turn the apple and, as you did this, it would peel the skin off of the apple. What an invention and labor saving tool! The result of this work was apple butter for the homemade bread—and that's a topic by itself (as we always fought for the end piece of the freshly baked loaf). The other delight the apples were used for were apple pies that were topped with that homemade ice cream mentioned above. We also canned tomatoes, beans, cabbage (kraut), and other vegetables found in our garden. The canned goods were used in the wintertime. No grocery shopping was required or coupons needed, as all we had to do was go into the cellar and pick from the shelves of filled Mason jars.

Social Events

Quilt-making was not only a necessity but was sometimes the centerpiece for a social event (sharing of news in the community sometimes referred to as "gossiping"). Competition for the best quilt was not only a social event but also a fund-raiser for the church or other charity organizations that raised money for the needy. These events were usually held on a Sunday afternoon. The entire family attended these competition and fundraising events.

Harvest time—what an event! Threshing time was tremendous. This was the time to bring in the wheat. Threshing crews would come to the farms with their big combines and farmers from all around would take turns helping one another to bring in their wheat crops. Everyone had a job, from the youngest to the oldest. You talk about teamwork—we had it all—motivation, objectivity, job satisfaction, equal opportunity, and yes, career path. Graduating from using a small pitchfork to a large pitchfork was what I call climbing the corporate ladder. The small pitchfork did not allow you to get the wheat onto the wagon and all of the hay fell down your shirt and that really did itch!

Now the food display was also a magnificent sight to behold. You have never seen such a "spread." I am talking—a good city block and a half! One section was vegetables, another meat, another pies, another all kinds of fruit and another drinks (mostly large pots of black coffee and, believe it or not, no one was nervous). The horses were unhitched and watered and the men folk lay down on the ground for about half an hour. Then we harnessed the horses, grabbed our pitchforks, and the crews started the big machinery. What a sight and what logistics! As I think back on the logistical efforts and organizational structure and communications, I remember that they were simple and workable. There were no corporate hidden agendas, no classes to take on motivation, teamwork or sensitivity training—just simple accomplishments by everyday folks who worked and lived together in harmony. How simple and beautiful and what a memory!

Another popular social event was the church picnic. People got together and enjoyed the food and fellowship in a wholesome environment. The games we played consisted of sack races, wheelbarrow races, ball games, and target shooting. Then there was the food competition, awarding cooks for the best pie or canned good, or other delightful concoction.

Rural America

This was how it was in rural America in the 30s and early 40s. For me particularly, the part of rural America in which I lived was Missouri. I was about nine or ten and was learning by example what family values meant. Some of these values, which were understood by the whole family, were prayers being said before meals and at bedtime, respect for others, and appreciation for the simple things in life. Materialism was not a priority, as there was happiness in having everyday necessities such as food, shelter and clean clothes on our backs.

Cleanliness was also a virtue. We took tub baths in a galvanized wash tub once a week in the kitchen. There was no running hot water (water was gotten from a well/cistern and we had to pump it up into a pail) so the water was heated on the kitchen wood stove. Now we worked outside and we got very dirty but it was clean dirt. Someone might say we were not too clean, but I say we were very clean. Even though we only took the tub bath once a week, we scrubbed up in the washbasin every morning, before meals, and before bedtime. The washbasin was a huge bowl, and we would fill it with water and use homemade soap. We definitely did not use store-bought soap. I don't remember the ingredients but the homemade bar was big and yellow and it took the dirt right off of your body without creating an enormous amount of soap lather. I remember smelling very clean.

A washtub and a "scrubbing board" were used for washing clothes. After the scrubbing was complete—and this was a very physical—task, the clothes were put into rinse water that had to be frequently changed. Now to complicate this even more, we had to empty the tub and get more water from the cistern. Getting water from the cistern was not automated but required the dropping of a bucket attached to a rope that was connected to a turn wheel that was manually operated. The system was – scrub, rinse, get more water from the well. The next step was to hang the wash on a clothesline. Now this was well and good in the summertime but when it was wintertime, the clothes being hung to dry would freeze. They were so stiff that I could almost walk alongside my "long johns" to bring them into the house. The stiff clothes were taken to the kitchen, the focal part of the home, and hung on all manner of devices to dry. They were not hung all at once because it was a several day process. They were hung near that famous wood burning stove. I must say, those stoves really generated a lot of heat. I remember the freshness of the clothes and again I attribute this to the homemade soap. It could very well be the same soap that we used in our weekly baths.

Later we upgraded our "washing machine" to one that had an agitator that was driven by hand. It also had a ringer attached that we could put the clothes through and get rid of the excess water, which made the item dry more quickly. I was the power behind the handle that turned the paddles. Now we have washers and dryers with the latest in technology. We also have Laundromats to handle our washing needs if our systems are shut down.

Inside plumbing was not available for my family and our neighbors but we did have the "outhouse" with the ever present and familiar Sear's Roebuck catalog. Normally the outhouses were made of wood, but there were some that were made out of brick. For those readers that used the old time outhouse there were many fears that came with the usage of this facility, which I will not write about. You can rely on your own memories or imaginations. Eventually, we did have a hand pump in the kitchen in order to pump water. The water was heated by setting the pan or bucket on the all-purpose wood burning stove. We used a washtub that was placed in the kitchen and the water was heated on the stove and poured into the tub. We washed using that homemade lye soap.

Coal oil lamps were the main source of light. We had no electricity. A lamp was used to guide the way to your room at night.

The lamp was used to read with and the main reading was from the Bible. We did not stay up late because we got up before dawn. Eventually electricity became available, which was revolutionary.

We did not have refrigerators and would put the dairy products in a bucket and lowered them into the cistern to keep cool. During the winter we had a wooden box that was kept on the porch, which would keep things cold but would not freeze. Now people in the city had wooden iceboxes that would hold the food and keep it cold by use of blocks of ice. The ice was put into a compartment at the top of the box that created the cold condition for the food. People would put a sign in the window for the amount of ice they wanted: 25, 50, 75 or 100 lb. Do you remember the need to check the drip pan to make sure the water did not go all over your shiny linoleum floor? Today we have refrigerators large and small, not only in our homes, but also on boats, airplanes, vans and so forth.

Today we not only have inside plumbing, some of the bathrooms even have Jacuzzi's and two washbowls. Some of the bathrooms today are as big as some of our bedrooms back in the good old days and also have the standard shower and bathtub. We also have multiple baths in some of our larger homes. Often, there are sunlamps placed over the washbowl to give you a "glow" during the wintertime.

A Few Other Tidbits from the Past

Let's start with the allowance that we were given as we grew up. The first allowance that I remember being given as a youngster (that was old enough to appreciate money) came from my uncle. He had a large farm and would give to each of the children a farm animal to raise and, at the appropriate time, the child would sell it and be able to keep the money. This was a great lesson in money management, for we learned what it takes to make a nickel. It's amazing today we have so many seminars on "Money Management." Then we had the traditional allowance, which was a quarter.

Another memory has to do with pets. I don't remember knowing anyone who had a purebred dog. The dogs I was aware of were the ones who brought the cows in from the field, would help keep rats off the property, would help when we went hunting and, I guess in summary, they all had a function to perform.

Remember reaching into muddy water to get a penny? Now I know everything is relative, as a newspaper only cost three cents, but the point is we went for it even if it was dirty.

I remember playing baseball without adult supervision. We did okay. We set the rules and time limits, chose sides and played the game without any interference from an adult. If we were not chosen as team members, we knew how to accept disappointment and we hung around anyway, watching the game, hoping that next time somebody would not show up and we would be picked to play on a team. To me that was the way to handle disappointment and develop character.

Remember filling stations that actually gave service? You got your windshield cleaned, oil checked, and gas pumped without asking, all for free, every time. And, you got trading stamps to boot. Today when I go to a full service station, I have to ask them to do this and I feel guilty as I may be imposing on them. But I do it anyway. You know us seniors.

When I grew up it was a safer time. No one ever asked where the car keys were 'cause they were always in the ignition of the car, and the doors were never locked. And you got in big trouble if you accidentally locked the doors at home, since no one ever had a key.

There was safety on the streets too. I remember in those days you could send a child to the store to buy a loaf of bread for fifteen cents and he would run home safely. I just wonder how many children today walk to the store to get that loaf of bread. I don't know, but from observation, I don't think there are many. In fact, I feel that a lot of young people do not know how to grocery shop.

Even with all our progress in technology, medicine, and science, don't you just wish, for once, you could slip back in time and savor the slower pace and share it with the children of today?

More Nifty Inventions

Remember the telephone on the wall with each resident having a certain number of rings? To call out, one would turn a crank by hand. I remember that families could have a community call and we didn't even know then about teleconferencing. Today we have many phones and lines in our homes. We have lines for our computers. We also have the cell phone that we use while shopping, driving the car, going to places of entertainment and even at lunchtime. What happened to lunches that were for eating and digesting your food and relaxing? Maybe the simpler times were better in some ways.

Coffee was made by putting coffee in a small sack and placing it in the big pot to let it boil or putting the coffee into the boiling water and then pouring it through a strainer for a good hot and strong cup of coffee. There were no electric toasters, no electric coffee pots, no waffle makers, no mixers, no George Forman grills, no blenders, no electric bread makers, no orange juice squeezers, no electric knives, no electric can openers, no electric or gas stoves or any of the other amazing electrical appliances. What did we have? A big black frying pan, big bowls for making bread and salads, wood burning stove, big heavy coffee pot, bread rollers and many more hand-held devices which were powered by a human being.

* * * * *

Historical Moment for 1938
Instant coffee is born. All you need is a cup of hot
water and a spoonful of Nescafé.

* * * * *

Cooking appliances in the past were primarily pans on top of the stove. The stove that I was familiar with when I lived in the country was the wood-burning stove, and when we moved to the city, we had a gas stove. There were no microwave ovens like today where you can cook a whole meal in a matter of minutes. Today we also have the option of buying a complete meal in the store and coming home and popping it into the oven. But I must say those meals can't match the home cooked meals that were made from scratch. What do I mean by "scratch?" Well, we would go out into the garden and pick some beans, peas, corn, potatoes from a potato mound, fresh strawberries and other berries, apples from the orchards, cherries from a tree which were very hard to get to, persimmons, cabbage, and the like. In the winter we used our canned vegetables that were contained in those aforementioned "Mason jars" and kept in the cellar. Bread was homemade, as were the butter and jellies. No appliances were used—just two hands and rolling pin, and two hands for kneading, then letting it rest, and proofing and putting it in the oven. No doubt in my case—those were two loving hands that belonged to a mom who took joy in providing food for the family. Today we have ready mixes that are put into a bread machine and, with the simple press of a button, you can get anything from white to wheat bread—and definitely no dough on the counter or hand labor required.

Floor carpeting was not seen in my community, but we did have 9' x 12' rugs that were used in the "special room" in the house. Now we did not have vacuum cleaners. So how did we clean them? We took them out and threw them over the clothesline and beat them with objects like a broom or other long-handled tool until the dirt was nonexistent, as far as the naked eye could see. Floor coverings were primarily wood or linoleum. We would scrub and clean them on our hands and knees. For the special room we would use floor wax to make them shiny after the good scrubbing. Today we have so many floor coverings available, like marble entrances in the foyer, carpeting all over the houses, different types of tiles and so many other coverings. Cleaning is not a problem. Vacuums are ever present, with some houses having central vacuum systems.

Liniment was used for sore backs and other aches and pains plus some other home remedies that worked that I can't recall. Compare that today with all kinds of appliances for our healthcare that we can use such as: electric foot massagers, seat cushions for the back and bottom, and even a device to strap on to your arms and legs to have a vibrating effect to relieve the soreness.

I have already mentioned dental hygiene, but one more item that required manual labor was that of shaving. We had straight razors with a brush and a shaving cup that contained soap. That's it— simple. Compare that to today's multitude of shaving devices, not only for the men but for the ladies as well. There are also electric toothbrushes (maybe that's not quite as painful as my grandfather's methods) and electric nose hair trimmers. Isn't it incredible what we think we can't do without?

Of course now we're spoiled on all these modern conveniences. When one breaks, we immediately replace it or repair it. Appliances are often given as gifts to family and friends for holidays and special occasions. This is nice, but I must say there were a lot of great things that were accomplished in the old days without these modern day appliances—like making bread by hand. Nothing compares to that taste and wholesomeness.

Chores

When it came time for chores, everyone had an assignment, even the very young ones. Before going to school, I had the responsibility to make sure the wood box was filled, including kindling wood. This was used to start the fire in the big black kitchen stove or, on occasions when there was "company" visiting, to start a fire in the wood stove that was in the front room. No one ever went into this room unless there was "company."

Other chores were outside. At planting time in the spring, we had a vegetable garden which supplied our daily meals. This was not a hobby but a critical part of being able to have fresh vegetables on the table. During the war, the term "Victory Garden" sprung up and even people in the cities started growing vegetables—something we had been doing as long as I remember. A chore for the youngster was that he was tied with a rope to a "garden plow" and someone else would put the blade into the dirt and together they would create a furrow in order to plant the seeds. An older and stronger person was pushing and guiding the garden plow and the youngster's job was pulling. This called for teamwork. When finished, the youngster was "un-harnessed" about the time when he heard the first bell ring at the country school. The school had two rooms with four grades in each room and each row in the room represented a grade, to the best of my memory. No, I did not have to walk ten miles to school, but when I tell this story to my grandkids, they are expecting that scenario.

Prayer and Bible Study

Prayer and reading from the Bible was also a part of our day. Prayers were said prior to each meal and, once the prayers were completed, the eating began. I was required to read from the Bible every night before going to bed. The light was dim because it came in the form of an oil lamp. To this day I remember certain readings from the "Good Book" that I learned "way back when." What a book to help formulate the foundation for a young person!

Entertainment

Do you remember the simple games you played as a child? I remember some of my children played the same games as I did, such as: marbles, kick the tin can and run, hide and go seek, elaborate snowball fights including the building of forts made out of snow, mumble peg, hoops (not basketball, but a round thin wheel pushed by a stick), and water balloon fights.

How about those 45 rpm records we had and dances like "cutting the rug," "jitter bug," "boogie woogie," along with our "jive talk?" For the younger reader, let me explain in more detail about the 45's. The record player had a post in the middle to keep the records all in line and then the records would drop down one at a time and off we went dancing to the next song until another record fell down and the music went round and round. We also had to dress the part with our pegged pants and dog chain. We guys had to have our hair slicked back, using red oil to grease the hair down. The girls were beautiful with their bobby socks and poodle skirts.

* * * * *

Historical Moment from 1950
This year's hit musical film *Singing in the Rain* stars
Gene Kelly and Debbie Reynolds.

* * * * *

Country Cookin'

Mealtimes were events due to the number and variety of foods that were prepared and consumed. Now you must remember, we grew our own food so did not have to go to the store to buy our groceries, except occasionally to buy salt, pepper and other like items. I remember one time buying a nickel's worth of bologna and it was approximately three inches high. It was a treat for the whole family—homemade bread with this store-bought lunch meat along with a big slice of onion. During the Depression we were blessed to have food on the table, unlike the people living in the city who had to stand in long lines to get just the basics that were often rationed. I remember when relatives came to visit

from the city they totally enjoyed the meals. I had an uncle and aunt who lived on their farm close by who had sixteen children. Yes, I said sixteen! When I visited, the table was filled with all kinds of food and nobody wanted for anything. I must say there was so much organization it was unbelievable. One age group was responsible for the next age bracket. What an example of how a large family worked together to have a wonderful family life! There were no conversations—nothing but the knives, forks and spoons hitting the plates and an occasional "pass me the whatever."

The one meal that was special for me was breakfast. I bet no king or queen had a meal like the one down on a typical farm. Homemade biscuits, fried potatoes, sausage, eggs, cream gravy, and homemade bread, butter and jelly were all served in abundance. I would finish my breakfast by putting three pieces of bread on my plate and covering them with gravy. What a meal!

I also remember how moms would teach their girls how to cook. To me cooking is an art. I have experienced the results of a mom's teaching her daughter how to cook. This example is my wife Betty. From the first day of our marriage she was an expert at cooking. There were homemade breads, biscuits from scratch, pork chop gravy, homemade apple butter and many other tasty things to delight the palate. By the way, she continues to cook but with a different menu appropriate to our age. Now I must say that in the early days of our marriage the magnitude of the meal also depended on how much money we had—which was good, as it continued to enforce the need to know how to manage our money. I am sure some of you readers can relate to that.

* * * * *

Historical Moment from 1948
Speedy new oven invented! Life in the kitchen just got easier with inventor Percy Spencer's new microwave oven.

* * * * *

Day's End

The day was always busy and, when it came to evening time, we all were very tired. We went to bed early and slept like a log. It was great sleeping when it was raining because we had a tin roof and we slept on goose feather mattresses. In the winter we did not move around too much as we had no heat in the room, so it was too cold to get out of bed. We dressed in the kitchen near the wood-burning stove.

Fleeting Youth

The word "resource" means: "A source of aid or support that may be drawn upon when needed." Today it is easy to criticize our young people because they are not like we were, but we need to realize that they are our greatest resource for the future. Not technology, science, intellectual assets, but the one thing I never hear anyone say when asked the question, "What is our greatest resource?"—the youth of our nation. What a God-given resource that we have, not only as a family, but as a nation. It is not enough to just criticize them—we must provide them direction in our social values and education, as they are the leaders of tomorrow. Without the proper raising of our youth, everything is irrelevant. They are the future engine that will drive the technology, sciences and trades. Along with this we must give them the greatest and that is encouragement.

We all need encouragement throughout our lives but let's make sure to especially encourage our youth, for they are laying the foundation for their lives.

I remember, as I am sure many of you do, when any of the senior members of the family spoke to us, we addressed them with respect and their proper title such as Uncle, Aunt and so forth. We also listened to them, as we respected their knowledge and knew that as children we did not know it all. Today, some of the new folks entering the business world seem to "know it all" and wonder when they are going to get a pay raise even before finding out where the rest rooms are (I'm exaggerating to make my point).

I feel that we must teach the younger members of our family to become excellent listeners. What encouraged me in the business world were the leaders who were outstanding listeners, regardless of one's status in the company. They were like sponges absorbing what was being said, and after much listening, they spoke of wisdom. I remember listening to every word. As time passed, I drew on the wisdom that I heard during those years and utilized those lessons in my day to day business. The same applies to the integrity of the outstanding people for whom I worked. Now this did not apply to all of them but the great ones had the kind of value system that was built on integrity.

Back in the '30s, '40s and '50s we had so many role models from our World War II heroes, our sports figures (who did not spit in the umpire's face or boxers who did not bite off part of their opponent's ear). How about our world leaders like Churchill and Franklin Delano Roosevelt? Even in the movies we had our heroes and role models like John Wayne and Greer Garson. These were role models that helped develop character for that generation of youth.

* * * * *

Historical Moment for May 25, 1935
American athlete Jesse Owens breaks five world records in one day.

* * * * *

So we were blessed in being exposed not only to our immediate family but those role models that we heard our family members talk about in a positive manner. For example, we had the opportunity to listen to people through President Roosevelt's fireside chats on our Zenith radio, with the whole family listening. We children were good listeners and that it is why when you go to a senior organization meeting today, as a rule, you hear prayer, the Pledge of Allegiance and the display of the American Flag. Now we as seniors have the responsibility to dialogue with our youth, for they truly are our greatest resource for the future.

There is much more to the day in the life of a youngster growing up in the rural areas that were very memorable but I will let you, the reader, reflect on memories that are yours alone.

CHAPTER THREE

Marriage

I deas of courtship and marriage have radically changed since the days of the '30s, '40s, and '50s. In many cases there is courtship without marriage (cohabitation) and marriage without courtship, and there is also a prevalent attitude that when things get rough in a marriage, it's time to get a divorce. The dating game rules have all changed, allowing dating services, Internet chat rooms, and TV game shows to be our guide to relationships. In our day, getting a date just happened naturally, without the aid of a third party enterprise.

Now having been married for 56 years, I feel qualified to speak on the subject. I have also observed the successful and long-lived marriages of many of my friends. We need to realize that there are cycles in marriages. There is the beginning of marriage that is totally out of this world, in terms of passion, commitment and enjoyment. There is the cycle of raising children, which requires the sharing of your time and love and attention. Then there is the period of time of financial challenges, (unless you are a person of "means"), affecting the career choices of both husband and wife. Finally, even retirement presents some challenges to a marriage, but throughout these years, the key word is *commitment*— to each other, to God, and to the institution of marriage because it is right. Throughout these challenging times and cycles of married life, we need to remember the lines we said when we took our wedding vows.

Do you remember that when at the altar of marriage you said the words "I do" you really meant it (the commitment, the "better or worse, sick or in health," etc.) and it was forever, rather than a temporary thing? It is very sad to look at current statistics on the rate of divorces. Divorce was rare in my day. The "I do" marriages experienced times of troubled waters but few left the boat. Instead, they stayed fast to the oars to get back to smooth sailing. Married life was built on give and take and divorce was not only frowned upon but not even a part of the vocabulary of most couples.

The Typical Family Today

There is no quick fix or single solution to what I consider a horrendous problem for this country. It took many decades to get where we are today with the crime, decline in morality, and the "do your own thing if it makes you feel good" attitude. It has taken decades for the breakdown of the family unit and it will take persistence and time to recapture it. We are not a society that sees things as being right or wrong. For instance, today this nation is starting to redefine what constitutes marriage. We have always defined marriage by the Judeo-Christian religion upon which this nation was founded. Back in the '30s and '40s, the Ten Commandments, good judgment and "horse sense" governed our lives. Now we are governed by "political correctness" and a wishy-washy value system that engenders mistrust, ambivalence, and a crumbling culture.

It is obvious that we need to return to our traditions and regain the stability that was evidenced in marriages in years gone by. Here are some thoughts on how we can bring back the "traditional" family.

First, the mother and father must decide and willingly agree that the materialistic success of the family unit is not the primary objective. There needs to be a time for the family to communicate on a regular basis, emphasizing the values that create lasting and loving relationships. This logically will result in a marriage that will grow. As the marriage grows in commitment and stability, there is a bonding by the entire family and love will be abundant. Without the stresses that come from always seeking more money, the mom and dad will have the time to observe, guide and apply corrective actions as required, using the "tough love" concept of raising children.

Secondly, we will have participation in school and community activities by the whole family. The correct concept of right and wrong in the home will have far-reaching results as it will influence other children who come to visit, allowing them to witness the joy and love shared by the family. This will result in behavior changes such as:

- Respect for the rule of law and authority, whether it is in educational institutions, community organizations, or the church environment.
- With the family being managed by the parents, the impact of certain outside influences that are negative to the children's behavior can be greatly reduced. This decision eliminates to a large degree the exposure of the children to much of the "trash" seen on TV and other media today.
- There needs to be a foundation for behaviors that will avoid discipline problems and in many cases criminal acts. For instance, a child may not even think of bringing a firearm into a school with the purpose of hurting another individual.
- The family will need to spend more time together. The divorce rate is going through the roof, but over time the decision to have more time together will reverse this trend. Why? Because, like anything, when you have success, it feels good and the success of the family unit is no different.

It is my belief that the preoccupation with material success is core to the break-up of the family unit. Our society as a culture is obsessed with materialism. This materialistic mindset leads to the "must have it now" attitude. The problem with this is that in order to have instant gratification for things that are outside the family budgetary limits, we must go into debt. This indebtedness puts a stress on the whole family, usually resulting in Mom going to work to help pay for these extra things. This in turn sets up a situation in which, when Mom comes home from work, she still is faced with fixing dinner, doing the wash and ironing and many more tasks. Preschool children are placed in day care centers, which means substitute mothers bring up the children. Children come home from school and there is nobody to greet them or make them those proverbial peanut butter and jelly sandwiches or help them with their homework. If we could get back to having the traditional family again, Mom would be at home in the afternoons, not only to provide those peanut butter sandwiches, but to give guidance as to who children's playmates would be, to monitor the TV watching, and to teach them values as she counsels them on various problems they might be having. Most of all, she would be *there.* She wouldn't have to go off to work feeling guilty for not giving her children enough "quality time." Now I realize that there are certainly many mothers that have to work these days, but I wonder how many more are just working in order to support a lifestyle that their families cannot afford. I am encouraged to see today that there is a growing trend of "working" moms who are leaving their careers in order to stay home with their children. This is a healthy sign that we may be beginning to turn the tide on the breakdown of the family.

Development of character of our children is the basic responsibility of the family unit. In her book, *It Takes a Village: And Other Lessons Children Teach Us* (Simon & Schuster Adult Publishing Group,1996), Hillary Clinton proclaimed, "It takes a village to bring up a child." However, I must disagree, as is stated by an Internet book reviewer named Blaine:

> This book is absolutely scary. For thousands (perhaps millions) of years, the family has been the basic building block of society. Now, we have a government (village) which, through heavy taxation and social-engineering has virtually destroyed the family and will continue to do so. And the best solution Clinton sees, is that very same government.[22]

A village is not required to develop character. This is one of the responsibilities of being a parent. Anyone can bring children into the world but it takes love and focus on the development of the child to enable him/her to be a good citizen, contributing to society in a positive way. Back in the '30s and '40s, as I was growing up, I can remember families instilling in the children the basic rules of our society, which in my case was based on religion. How was this being done? First of all there was a family consisting of Mom and Dad and the children. These parents started lessons with the children at a very early age. Sharing was taught. In order to instill the value of truthfulness in a child, even little "fibs" were unacceptable. Cheating was also not acceptable. Work ethics were instilled, as all of the children had "chores" that were given based on their ages and abilities. The quality and timeliness of the respective chore was also important such as: making sure the wood was brought into the house before we left for school; cutting the grass before we went to play; straightening our rooms before we went outside, etc.

Teamwork was recognized at a very early age. One of the opportunities that was provided me at an early age was working as part of the farmer's team to bring in the harvest. Even at the age of eight I was required to pitch hay (my grandfather made me a wooden pitch fork so that I could handle the "pitching hay" chore), attempting to get the hay from the ground to the wagon and eventually to the barn. Did the hay make it to the wagon? Not really, but the hidden agenda of my uncle was to build a work ethic as well as being a part of the team. To me this is part of character building.

Another main ingredient of building character is teaching respect—respect for your elders, respect for the law, respect for your teachers, respect for your country, respect for the military and all those in authority. This was a given when as I was growing up.

It is even more important in our day that we practice these teachings. This will contribute to the building of the foundation for the men and women of the future, who will be the leaders that will determine the kind of society in which we will live. I must say that we must reach into the past to reaffirm that character does count. The idea that cheating and lying are okay as it relates to your private life, as long as you were doing your job, is ludicrous and unacceptable. Instead of spending so much time and energy trying to justify our lack of character, let us build the character of our young people, preparing them to take over the leadership for the future. Development of character is accomplished by teaching, being role models, correcting as appropriate and continuing to monitor the child as he grows into a responsible adult.

A family is a single unit in society and it will take many, many units together deciding that materialism is not the primary objective of our lives and to help us return to sanity and setting the correct priorities. In other words, we will build a cultural change in society one family at a time.

In my day, the family environment was one filled with morality, discipline, respect, and assigned responsibilities and, without question, everyone knew and accepted his/her role.

Another characteristic of this family had to do with their attitude toward managing money. For example, we used public transportation until we saved enough to buy a car—in my case as a twenty-two-year-old, a car that cost four hundred dollars and was in continual need of fixing. We were patient, and when we were able to buy that "widget" whatever, the whole family was overjoyed. I guess these days we are not as appreciative and thankful for these material blessings. We looked forward to working overtime so that we could buy some essentials (note, I said *essentials*) that the family needed. Sure, we wanted extra stuff, but we did not have to have instant gratification as today.

Another thing about this traditional family was that they did things together, such as going to church and school events or to a theater to see two movies with a cartoon and the news. Going together to these events meant that no baby-sitters were required. Do you remember when it was parent-teacher night at school and both parents and their children would go to meet with the teachers and tour the schoolrooms? Do you remember looking at the pictures on the walls in the hallway the children had drawn, searching for your own child's drawings? Remember anticipating what the teacher would have to say about your child's progress (or lack thereof) and asking what you as parents could do to help? It seems that today that an honest evaluation about your children is often unwelcome. There is the attitude that there is nothing wrong with our little darlings, but if they are performing poorly it must be because the teacher is failing. When my wife and I were raising our children, we (and I think a majority of parents) were willing to work as a team with the teacher to help our children succeed. There were certain issues that needed to be addressed, and when the issue was resolved, we were so thankful that our child had the privilege of being taught by this teacher who was really an educator. It turned out to be an enjoyable evening as we met some of our neighbors and their children and had a chance to visit with them briefly. Afterward we would go to the school gym and have refreshments, and in our case, we finished the evening outing by walking home together. It is amazing how the accumulation of little wonderful happenings as you raise a family become the foundation of your memories.

A Typical Day in the Life of...

What are some other "little" things which we remember about family life in the '30s, '40s, '50s, and even early '60s? Mornings would start very early. Children were awakened. In those days, we did not have one and a half or two and a half baths, but rather one small bathroom that was used by all. Pecking order for the use of the bathroom started with Mom. She was always the first one to get up and put the coffee pot on, start breakfast, ad prepare the lunches for the day for Dad and the children. When I was a child, we didn't carry lunch in a brown bag—it was in a pail. Next in the bathroom was Dad so he could get ready for work. It was only then that the children got the bathroom, in descending order with the oldest first. They all arrived at the breakfast table at the same time, except for the youngest—they were the trailers and often heard Mom yelling, "Breakfast is ready and your food will get cold!" They all knew that they did not want to get two such calls because the next step was for Dad to intervene. This would not be a call, but rather footsteps coming down the hall and we knew that the outcome would not be desirable.

After breakfast, Dad was off to work while Mom was making sure the children were properly groomed, their lunches packed and, as they left the house, instructions were given to the oldest to look after the younger children. Some of these instructions were things like, "Wait for your brother or sister and come home together," or "No dilly-dallying on the way home." Now they didn't always come home together due to different extracurricular activities such as band or sports. But Mom knew these schedules, as she was very much aware of all the activities in which her children were involved. So as the children were leaving the house in the morning, confirmation of activity schedules were discussed. Mom would say, "You have band today? What time is band over? So you should be home at this time? Correct?" and child would answer, "Yes, Mom." It was pure old-fashioned communication. If there was a variation in the schedule, they had to have a reason.

So the children were off to school and husband was off to work, so now what did the mom do at home all day? Well, to start with, she probably had one or more preschool- aged children to care for and then there were the household chores like washing, cleaning, grocery shopping, and cooking dinner. However, periodically during the week, the ladies would get together and have coffee and cake and discuss a whole range of topics. For the mothers who had roles in the Girl Scouts, Boy Scouts, PTA and other like organizations, these activities had to fit into their already busy schedules.

Now it was time for Dad to come home. He walked up the sidewalk and approached the front door of his "palace," waiting to be greeted by the family, as was a daily ritual. Mom had already primped up for Dad's arrival—yes, moms primped to greet their husbands. He entered and received a big hug. Mom then started giving instructions for the family to assemble. Dinner was not only the time for eating but also for family exchange of what happened in each one's life that day. It usually started with Mom, followed by Dad and then down into the ranks of the children. After dinner (by the way, no one was excused from the table until everyone was done eating) Mom would start the dishes with the help of the children. As this process was going on, Dad was having a one-on-one with the children. He would look at their homework and review it and, if it was bad, it was redo time. Other discussions were held concerning anything the child might have on his/her mind. Now one might say this was like a prison and this was not a common routine for most families. Well! I am here to say that my personal experiences were that this was the routine for the majority of families I knew who were everyday working people. Everyone in the family knew they were loved. I remember a conversation between a father and his youngest son one evening after dinner. The father was telling his son about driving the car and the things not to do and things he should do. The conversation had gone on for quite some time and the son finally said to his father, "Dad, why are you always picking on me?" The father reflected for a minute or so and replied, "Because I love you and if I didn't care I would not be talking to you." The son instantly replied, "Would you please not love me so much?" As we all know, parenting is a full time job with roles for everyone.

Dinner over, chores done, and discussions completed, the family would all head for the front yard to enjoy the closing of the day. Now one of the main reasons for going out of the house was because it was hot and we didn't have air conditioning and the outside afforded us the opportunity to cool off. Families would exchange greetings. Dads would exchange conversations as well as the moms with the neighbor ladies. Children would play with the neighborhood children and it truly was like a scene out of a movie starring Donna Reed and Jimmie Stewart. I know it to be true because I was there, just like so many of the people that are reading this as well as the people I have talked to after one of my speeches. Winter time was the same except the family would get together in the front room and when "company" would visit, the children's friends would go to their rooms to play and the grown-ups would visit in the kitchen with a hot cup of coffee.

The nightly routine at bedtime was to say prayers and then lights out, and the parents' giving a good night kiss and saying, "Go to sleep. See you in the morning." Mom and Dad would go downstairs and turn on the Zenith radio and listen to the "Green Hornet," "Gangbusters" or some like program. While the programs were on, Mom read a magazine or filled out an eagle stamp book while Dad read the paper.

I am sure, for some of you, as you have read this, it has brought back many more memories of those days gone by. It is my opinion that they were great. We didn't have all of the technology, ice machines, air conditiong, two cars, two garages, etc. that we have today. But we also didn't have to lock the doors to the house, we could sleep in the park overnight, not worry about the children getting shot when they went to school, not reading the paper about another sex scandal involving our elected officials, nor reading of the sports page about athletes being arrested on drug charges or other crimes, nor worries about ratings at the movies, nor television problems, for there were none.

Social Values

It is easy to be pessimistic about our society but I think we can be optimistic knowing that there are young people who uphold the social values we treasure. Our nation is above approach when it comes to the advances made in medicine, the sciences and technology but it is my opinion that we are among the leaders of the world when it comes to the decline of societal values. What are some of these values of which I speak?

- Respect for persons or property
  A lack of respect results in crimes such as murder, rape, white-collar crimes, thievery, and now, identity theft.

- Honesty and Integrity
  There is much fraud and deception by some of the corporate executives in companies. Every weekend I hear on the radio this week's list of companies who have allegedly committed some act of deception for the purpose of misleading someone for personal profit

- Morality
  As I have touched on so many times, it is my opinion that we are continuing to have a rapid decline of morality in this country. Some examples of this decline of morality can be seen in all its repulsiveness through musical entertainment, television, and magazines. Movies have ratings for the

purpose of providing guidance on what age group can see that particular movie. Now think about that—if I as an adult can go see an "R" rated movie (as evidenced by advertising this movie that it contains sex, nudity and violence) and I am supposed to be setting an example for the younger people, then I am a hypocrite. If I want them to have higher moral standards, I must have them myself. Seniors today are appalled at this slide in morality, and more than that, the seeming unconcern of many toward it. I believe this slide began somewhere around the sixties, but really accelerated in the nineties. We of the senior set are still highly sensitized to these things, and we need for our voices to be heard.

- Medical Care
Who cares that we have lost the traditional family doctor? I want to go back in time and tweak your memories when our doctors would make house calls and there was the term "family doctor" had true meaning. These family doctors knew the entire family's medical history. But today, we seniors have to make decisions on who our doctor will be due the insurance companies they recognize. I am aware of many war stories when it comes to this subject. We have a friend who had good insurance but her doctor moved to a new insurance plan and she followed. Her doctor did a hip replacement under the old plan, which cost a minimal amount. She had to have the other hip operated on utilizing the new plan and it cost her approximately $3000. She now has a dilemma in deciding whether she should go back to the old plan, which is less expensive, or stay with her doctor, utilizing the more expensive plan. This lady is not rich and she does not need these problems in the twilight of her years. Yes, I hear all the politicians talk about health care but I ask, "Do they really care?" The next time you get the chance, ask them about their health insurance plans. If they had to have the same plans that we have, they would get off of the proverbial "pot" and do something about it.

Bringing Up Baby

Admittedly, parenting is a tough job. And many still do a good job of parenting, in spite of the decline of values. We who have raised children have all experienced the "worrying life cycle," with perhaps a few exceptions. It all starts when the wife becomes pregnant. The future parent has the sometimes hidden and sometimes outwardly concerns of "I hope the baby is okay" and "Is Mom okay?" Then there are the concerns of others, asking, "How are you feeling? Are you walking? Are you taking your vitamins? What did the doctor say?" This is love in the form of concern and sometimes worry.

More questions arise after the baby is born that concern the baby's well-being according to statistics relative to when the child should be walking, eating solids, weight, height, and other vital statistics. Yes, some do worry about these matters, which I feel is a normal thing for loving parents.

Then, as the child gets older, Dad may get a phone call like this: "Sam, come home—Jr. just ran into a concrete wall. Should we take him to the doctor?" Dad rushes home and everyone gets into the family car and are off to the doctor, who sees the family immediately. It is nothing major—just a few stitches and it's all over. As the parents are driving home, the worry is expressed about Jr.'s ability to reach manhood without killing himself. (Note: Jr. grew up to be a well-coordinated and healthy man.).

Now we have reached school age and the parents attend a parent-teacher meeting held in the classroom of their child. The teacher now starts telling them that their child has been given the affectionate name by the teacher of "Sunshine" because he is very disruptive in the class as he is consistently talking and being the "ambassador" of goodwill. The parents express concern as they see their child's potential career path as one of total disaster. The teacher replies, "Don't worry. He is going through a growing-up phase." The parents accept this but keep an eye on this aspect of his growth.

Then before you know it, Jr. is asking for the car keys so he can take the car out on his own. To me, this was the most challenging time of parenthood. Worry is all over the place. Dad has told his soon to be an adult son to be home at a certain time. The curfew time comes and the driver is not home. Now anxiety attacks set in as the clock ticks. Fifteen minutes pass, half an hour passes and finally the young adult strolls into the house totally unconcerned. Dad is up and in the face of the first-time driver who just violated the trust of his parents by not being on time in his solo flight. The driver states that he was talking to a friend and time escaped him. The explanation satisfies the parents' need for the infraction but they now go into the lecture about the "worry" they had for their first-time driver whom they love so very much. In their minds, they had all types of disastrous scenarios. Worry! Worry!

Can it be that parents are sentenced to a lifetime of worry? Is concern for one another handed down like a torch to blaze the trail of human frailties and the fears of the unknown? Is concern a curse? Or is it a virtue that elevates us to the highest form of life? It is my opinion that this is not a curse but rather a sign of love.

This virtue is passed onto our children. Recently, we had lunch with one of our children and we stated we were on our way home after lunch so we could complete some work. Well! As we were on our way home, we decided to stop in at a friend's house for a brief visit. The child (now a married lady with grown children) who had just had lunch with us called our house. We obviously were not home. Several hours passed and she still could not get us. As we drove up to our house after our visit with the friend, there were cars all over the place. The daughter had called her brothers and they all were at the house ready to break down the door and call the police regarding their missing parents. They were all very irritable, saying, "Where were you guys? We were worried. Don't do that again."

Of course we were sorry that we gave them a concern but I must confess it was great to see the worry that was expressed that was a product of their love. I guess we passed on that legacy of love.

Tough Love

Sometimes parenting calls for tough love. Tough love is a very descriptive way to express decisions that parents had to make in the past and is a concept that is needed even more today.

This kind of love is not only for the sake of the children but also society as a whole.

What is tough love? I can best describe it by relating an experience of this father whom I know very well. His son was an excellent athlete and also a very intelligent person. One would say that he was blessed with natural abilities. He took a barrage of physical and mental tests, which he passed and was accepted by the Air Force Officer Training program. Time passed and one night his father received a call from his son, who immediately went into a whole list of reasons why he wanted his father to come and get him out of the program. Ha! As if his father could do that! The reasons for his wanting out were they were giving him too many things to learn, they had him up in the middle of the night doing training, and the pressure was too great. The father listened very closely, and as he listened, he became very sympathetic to his son's plea for intervention and escape from this supposedly "hell" on earth. The son finished and the sympathetic father almost made a mistake by agreeing with the son. But something intervened in the father's thought process and this is what came out, "What in the heck is this all about? You're an athlete and you are intelligent and not a quitter. Well son, I want you to stick it out and give it the very best. How can this be so rough when tens of thousands have gone through this training before you arrived? I never want a call like this from you again because you are a winner and I want you to try like 'heck.' Just give it your very best. That is all anybody wants from you." Well, graduation came and the family was very proud as they stood there on the Air Force parade grounds watching all the young and beautiful people receiving their commissions as second lieutenants in the United States Air Force. But that's not the end. The son not only graduated but also was first in his class. That night after the phone call to his dad and his father was tough with his son, the father did not sleep all night but prayed to the Almighty to give his son the strength and the wisdom to do what he was totally capable of doing. The father's tough love and prayers resulted in the son's success.

Today parents are faced with many tough love decisions—decisions about their health, (such as not smoking or doing drugs), attitude towards school and friends, issues regarding driving the car, issues regarding sex, obscene language, and entertainment as a whole. Parents must be the role models for their children, not the entertainment industry and our political leaders. This requires tough love as the peer pressure for the children of today. Know the friends of your children and look into their social activities. Tough love is a full-time job for both parents.

Tough love is just another action that demonstrates your concern and interest in your child. This is more important than anything materialistic that might be given to a child. Often, things are substitutes for time and love. The reason that tough love is so valuable is that the child recognizes you really cared to provide him a proper direction for his path in life. We are blessed to be parents and we must accept our responsibilities of full-time parenthood in providing direction and love, which sometimes is very tough on all parties.

Moms

So many things have been written about moms but I can't help but write about the moms that I have known in my lifetime. To me, moms are the heart of the family. They are the ones who have the patience, understanding and time to be a good listener, regardless of how busy they are and how poorly they may be feeling at that given point. You can see the compassion in their eyes and hear it in their tone of voice.

Moms are still moms, even if they are the "grand-" moms or "great grand-" moms. Their roles are relative to the "pecking" order in the family unit but sometimes the grand- and great grand-moms are all called to active duty if Mom is absent for some reason. Why? Because we are family.

I remember my grandmother who was always there for me. She was the enforcer when it came to scrubbing behind my ears, filling the wood box, reading a chapter of the Bible, saying my prayers and getting to bed on time. In addition to this, she was the nurse who put medicine on my cuts, reviewed my home work, patched my clothes, and made sure I did not have a "cow lick" on the back of my head before I went to school. As a youngster I helped her in the "truck garden," growing vegetables for our table. She not only was my grandmother but she was my friend and I owe her for the solid foundation she gave me as a young boy.

Now I see firsthand another mom whom I have known for over fifty-six years. To this day, after four children, seven grandchildren and soon to be five great-grandchildren, she is still a mom. What duties do I see her perform? She is the spiritual leader of the family, sending readings, poems and articles to all family members periodically. She has true concern for the family, even in the early hours of the morning when someone is sick. She's still a baby-sitter, and is in attendance at all births. The house still maintains dolls and toys for the visits by the children. Everybody is remembered on the holidays. Most importantly, her love comes from her heart as she attends to the family's needs—a love that is consistent from day to day.

I notice this in other grandmoms, as this is our primary circle of friends at this cycle of our "mature" life. It is great to witness, as they truly are the cornerstones of the family.

Time marches on and what do I see? I see the new moms of the family. It's great. Life is starting again for the new moms, who I know will continue the tradition of being the loving listeners, caring, patient, enforcers and spiritual nurturers of the family because they were taught by the "very best"—the grand- and great-grandmoms.

Then and Now

As I look back at my growing up years, I just don't know how we survived and are still on this earth. Maybe it was only by the grace of God. I remember riding in the rumble seat of the models A and T Ford, going down a gravel road and not having an air bag or seat belt. Yes, we weren't going that fast but those roads were not exactly as smooth as the roads of today. How about riding in the back of a pickup truck? Not just one person, but sometimes there were maybe four or five. I remember going with a group of children in the pickup to see an outside movie and this was before the drive-in theaters. We went there, watched and returned home. We were not strapped in and, looking back, I don't know how we survived.

We did not have all of the vitamins that we have today. At least, if they were available, my community did not know about it. We did not have all of the energy bars, drinks, and health foods. But we did have fresh food grown in our gardens. We did not have the annual checkups or pre-school exams, but we survived. I think a lot of this was due to our environment's being more pure than we have today. We did not have all of the junk food that we have today. So logically, we did not need all of today's "life support items."

I don't know how we survived because we did not have the health clubs of today. We did not have the diet experts. We did not have the bicycle clubs and the list goes on. These things of today are good because they support today's lifestyle. We got our exercise from doing chores and hard work. We got our physical workout by walking every place. We did not have to worry about calories because we did not have junk food. For example, we had an apple from a tree, blackberries from a bush, and grapes from a vine. Maybe that's why we did not have many cavities in our teeth (which was fortunate considering our "dentist" was the blacksmith).

I just don't know how we survived. We drank water from a cistern. I even chewed "road tar" as a gum substitute. Think about that one! Would you consider doing that today? I don't think so.

After I had moved to the city, on Saturdays I would leave early in the morning to play baseball all day. I would get home in time to eat a sandwich and then go to my job as an usher at the Union Theater.

As a parent I remember that we had little league tryouts for our children and not everyone made the team. But those who did not make the team had to learn what disappointment was all about. I am sure that some of you readers may not think this was fair, but it is my opinion that this helps a child in developing character. I have experienced disappointment and what it did for me was to make me more determined to overcome that failure that led to disappointment. There are a lot of alligators out there, so you had better be ready to handle them. I survived.

As far as school is concerned, some students weren't as smart as others or didn't work hard, so they failed a grade and were held back to repeat the same grade. Today it is common for students in higher grades to have problems with the basics, such as reading, writing and arithmetic—if that is still the baseline—and they continue to be promoted to the next grade. It seems the schools are afraid of the parents' wrath if their "precious children" don't get promoted. Remember when being sent to the principal's office was nothing compared to the fate that awaited a misbehaving student at home? Basically, we were in fear for our lives, but it wasn't because of drive-by shootings, drugs, gangs, etc. Our parents and grandparents were a much bigger threat! But we all survived because their love was greater than the threat.

That earlier generation produced some of the greatest risk takers and problem solvers—like Thomas Edison, who invented or improved upon the telephone, the gramophone, the electric light, the battery, and motion pictures.* Other risk takers of that generation of adults were Franklin Roosevelt as he instituted a job program by the government to provide jobs for those affected by the Great Depression.* There were women risk takers too, like Amelia Earhart who made history by being the first person to fly solo nonstop for 16 hours across the Atlantic.* And then there were the just for fun creations like comic books and superheroes Batman, Superman, and Wonder Woman (1930s and 1940s), the game called Monopoly (1934) and the cartoon character Donald Duck (1934).*

How about this memory and how we survived? We would spend hours building our go-carts out of scraps and then rode down the hill, only to find out we forgot the brakes. After running into the bushes a few times, we learned to solve the problem. To slow down the go-cart we had to drag our feet. To create a brake was quite an invention—all done with wood, nails and a couple of screws. The bad part was this was done on city side streets and, sometimes in order to stop the cart, we had to hit the curbing instead of a bush. I really don't know how we survived. We used to go "sleigh riding" on a hill in the park on a piece of cardboard and ice skating without knowing how to skate, being totally embarrassed by constantly falling. I knew the ceiling better than any other part of the arena! But we survived.

We had no childproof lids on medicine bottles, doors, or cabinets, but we knew how to keep these from the children. We also did not have any bars on the windows or doors and we survived.

Community

It seems to be that back in the '30s and '40s, we not only had both parents in the home supervising us, but the whole community got in the act. Remember the closeness of the community when you were about to do something really bad—like trying to be an adult and light up a cigarette? The chances were you would run into the football coach, or the nosy neighbor (a childhood term for someone who would "tattle tale" to our guardians on our infraction of the family rules). Or it might have been somebody from church or a buddy's little sister. All of them knew your parent's phone number and your first name. It was a good thing because it helped us realize we were accountable for our actions, and these were people who cared enough for us that they set the boundaries. Also, it seemed to me that family generally lived in the same neighborhood or home-town with their relatives. And when it came to child care this meant grandparents or aunts or uncles.

Remember when you could go to the barbershop and get a hair-cut, a shoeshine and a manicure? You could also get a shampoo and a shave with a straight razor. The only thing remaining today is getting a haircut and a wonderful conversation with your barber. If you are lucky, the shop will have people waiting and everyone has an opinion about a common subject such as sports and some local issues. If not engaged in conversation, I know I have gotten to the stage in life when sometimes I take a "cat nap." I am always surprised that I was still upright in the chair. Those naps are refreshing.

Seniors – Our Heroes

Just think about it. Seniors have all come a long way on a road that at times was very bumpy. Let's start with the Great Depression. There were no jobs. Some folks found it hard to get a meal and would do chores such as cutting wood to even have their basic needs met. Any type of work would do. The government established CCC camps for people to work on the highways and so forth in order to put food on the table. For the young and uninformed, CCC stands for Civil Conservation Corp. Some of the farms experienced droughts in certain parts of the country. There was the migration of families to different parts of the country in order to find work. But they survived because they were a generation that was very resolute.

Our generation went through the horrors of World War II. It began on a Sunday morning, December the 7th 1941, when our nation was plunged into war by a sneak attack on Pearl Harbor by the Japanese.

Our nation was not prepared for another war on this scale. But it did not take long for the nation to rise to the occasion. Men and women joined the armed forces. The draft was implemented. There were men who were drafted for their skills regardless of age or physical fitness. The women were also there to join by enlisting in the WAC's (Women's Army Corps). These were the women who ferried the planes to England in support of the Air Force. A merchant marine force was established and there was the tremendous build-up of the armed service medical staff.

On the home front, there were dynamic changes to the lifestyle. We were just coming out of the Depression when we were forced to adjust again to a traumatic event. The war effort was huge. At the beginning, the army had trucks on which they would hang a sign on the side of the truck saying "tank." That is just one example of how unprepared our military was for a war—not just a war, but a world war that covered Europe, the Pacific and Asia.

* * * * *

Historical Tidbit from 1940
A new vehicle being used by the army is
the Willys General Purpose Vehicle
(jeep, for short – designed for battlefield reconnaissance).
It is an all-terrain vehicle that can go up to 65 miles per hour.

* * * * *

Rosie the Riveter was introduced into our vocabulary. Plants sprung up all over the country to provide the ammunition, equipment, planes, ships and other supportive supplies. The military had to become logistics experts to support the war fronts.

In addition to the ordinary folks that came from all over the country to join the service and the folks left behind, there is another category of those who served whom I would like to mention. These were (believe or not) the movie stars. There were some famous (or after the war became famous) movie stars who immediately signed up without waiting to be drafted. Now in my opinion they were no greater than the farm boy or others who immediately enlisted but I mention them because I admired them both for their acting and their willingness to serve.

So let's go back in time to generate some memories about some of the stars that we loved to watch on the screen but in addition share with you some facts about their new live "roles" in World War II. Did you know that James Stewart (of "Mr. Smith goes to Washington") flew 20 missions as a B-24 pilot in Europe? I don't believe he stammered in his speech when he was flying over Germany. How about the "Gone with the Wind" star Clark Gable, who went on to serve as a waist gunner flying missions on a B-17 in Europe. George C. Scott, who played the part of the great General Patton in the movie "Patton" was a US Marine. That was good casting! Charlton Heston, the star of "The Ten Commandments," was an Army Air Corps Sergeant in Kodiak. And Eddie Albert, the star of the TV series "Green Acres," was awarded a Bronze Star for his heroic action as a U.S Naval officer.

There were many more but I can't list them all here. I just want to say they are to be admired for the roles they played on the screen as well as the service they offered, along with millions of other men and women, to help us win the war against the Axis powers.

In addition the celebrities that joined the USO and entertained the troops all over the world. We must especially mention Bob "Thanks for the Memory" Hope, who thrilled millions of our Armed Service personnel. Isn't great to be an American? How blessed we are!

Then there were the ones who experienced the sadness of losing loved ones in the war. Gold stars were put in the windows of homes where family members who were in the war gave the ultimate sacrifice for their country. The dreaded message "killed in action" was devastating for all. It has been over sixty years but some seniors of today still remember the telegram being delivered. There was a deluge of telegrams after the Allies hit the beachhead on Normandy and the other beaches. Even today the veterans that served in World War II still have vivid memories of those days. Not only the veterans but also their wives suffered so much, not knowing the safety of their loved ones. What a tremendous burden they had to carry. But you know what? I have never seen such patriotism as today's seniors showed during that wartime era. We did not even think about burning the flag. Everybody bought war bonds and the ten-cent stamp books. We seniors should remind the youth of today about those heroes of that time in our country's history. Some of the veterans of that time also served in Korea and again were called on to serve in a war far away. This again created suffering for many of our citizens. Many of those heroes are not here to tell us of their sacrifices but many are living today. They are called "senior citizens."

CHAPTER FOUR

The Senior Years

B ack then we appreciated the simple things of life. When we are young we tend to take everything for granted, and that is reasonable because we are busy growing and learning about life. Everything is new and a mystery and we are constantly in the process of digesting this input and making decisions about the future and other things that may have an impact on our lives.

This learning continues at varying degrees as we mature, whether we are single, entering the work force, getting married, becoming a parent, becoming a grandparent, then a great-grandparent and, in some cases, great-great-grandparent.

Life has its cycles as we can all attest to and we are absorbed with living out those cycles. Now to the point that I want to make. Along this highway of life, we are so busy growing and taking care of business that we don't stop to smell the flowers. Maybe that is left for the mature citizens so we finally have the opportunity to stop and think about the simple things of life, of which there are many.

Have you ever really looked at a flower and noticed the beauty? Or the bees that extract the nectar, which sustains their lives? Birds in flight are wondrous to watch as they work feverishly to build their nests, protecting and feeding their young. How about the ants and their busyness?

Have you ever taken a walk on the beach as the sun was rising with the quietness of the morning? Your ear is attuned to the slap-slap of the waves on the shore and your face is refreshed by the sweetness of the breeze. Your bare feet touch the sand and the sky provides a blue backdrop displaying beautiful billowing clouds. How divine is this simple experience of life! Maybe we as mature citizens are blessed in that our minds are not complicated with everyday living so that we can see these simple things that nature provides. To me it is cleansing.

How about a walk in the park or the woods, which provides a different beauty but is just as rewarding, especially in the spring and fall of the year? Many people travel to the northeastern part of the United States to observe the flaming color of the plentiful trees during the fall season of the year.

Appreciation for the simple things helps us understand what life is all about. It is the simple surroundings that are free for all of us to enjoy and provide us varying degrees of contentment and happiness during this cycle of our lives.

So enjoy the multitude of simple things that we are given without any cost, and you will derive some degree of happiness. Besides watching the things that Mother Nature provides us, take notice on how our babies sleep in all innocence and purity. Notice when they are hungry, when they are playing with their toys—oh, what a sight to watch! Sometimes you will catch yourself smiling, which is a great indicator that the simple things of life truly make you happy.

We had the freedom, failure, success and responsibility, and we learned how to deal with it all and we survived. Yes, we of the generation of the Great Depression and World War II knew how to be survivors, for we learned to do without when we had to and fought hard to succeed in spite of the obstacles. They were "years of struggle" in many ways, but also years of great joy as we remember our childhood days and young parenting days. We got a firm foundation on which to build our lives by embracing the high moral standards of the Christian faith and the solid social values of a nation united "under God."

Who will be this generation's geniuses, explorers, inventors, and leaders? We could look around us and be discouraged, wondering if this generation of young people will have the strength of character and firm value system that will help them survive. But be encouraged. Senior citizens still have a vital role to play in society. We as seniors can help determine what foundation young people are laying for future success. Granddads and Grandmoms, do all you can to teach and encourage your children, grandchildren, and great-grandchildren. They will learn those value systems we have by watching and listening to us. So I guess if you want to know how to define the family, that last statement about sums it up.

* * * * *

S M I L E

The Perks of Being 50+

1. Kidnappers are not very interested in you.

2. In a hostage situation you are likely to be released first.

3. No one expects you to run—anywhere.

4. People call at 9 pm and ask, "Did I wake you?"

5. People no longer view you as a hypochondriac.

6. There is nothing left to learn the hard way.

7. Things you buy now won't wear out.

8. You can eat dinner at 4 pm.

9. You enjoy hearing about other people's operations.

10. You have a party, and the neighbors don't even realize it.

11. You get into heated arguments about pension plans.

12. You no longer think of speed limits as a challenge.

13. You quit trying to hold your stomach in, no matter who walks into the room.

14. You sing along with elevator music.

15. Your eyes won't get much worse.

(Source Unknown)

* * * * *

1940-1949
"Wars and Rumors of Wars"

Almost all the news reports in 1941 had to do with the US involvement in World War II. Hitler was on the rampage, persecuting and systematically killing the Jews in Germany and throughout Europe and persecuting Christians who helped the Jews in what would become known as the Holocaust; Japan attacked Pearl Harbor; the economy became ever more centered around the war effort. In 1943, President Franklin D. Roosevelt imposed a freeze on prices and wages in the US.

In 1945, the US dropped atomic bombs, weapons of unusual destructive power, on Japan. President Truman was the Commander in Chief to make that decision. On May 8, 1945 victory was declared in Europe. In 1949, NATO, the North Atlantic Treaty Organization was formed.

On the home front, with the War ending, the economy made a shift away from defense to production of goods for consumers, setting the stage for prosperous times to come. The mood was light as our soldiers came home from war duty and started their families. Americans were ready for better times and this was reflected in the world of entertainment, business, and inventions. An example of innovating inventions from 1947 was the development of a tiny device that could control an electrical current and amplify it. It was known as a transistor and would transform the world of radio broadcasts.

As in the 1930s, the 1940s produced a bumper crop of more survivors. The men and women who lived through World War II would never be the same again, and they are among the most patriotic US citizens today. Nothing can create appreciation for the blessing of freedom like having the threat of that blessing being taken away.

SECTION 2

TREASURED FRIENDS
AND MORE

CHAPTER FIVE

Friendship

The dictionary defines a friend as "A person you know well and regard with affection and trust." What a blessing to have friends, especially if you have one true friend you feel you can call upon anytime. There are a few friends upon whom I can call that I can ask with confidence, "Would you do me a favor?" ad their replies will always be, "Yes, how may I help you?" I don't know about you but that makes me feel happy all over, not because the person is going to do me a favor, but because my subconscious is telling me once more how lucky I am to have a friend. Many times we measure our blessings by material goods, but the value of a true friend can't be measured. A friend is a special treasure that brings a certain contentment. This kind of friend is someone you trust wholeheartedly, and with whom you can totally be yourself.

This trust must be earned and it only comes over time as friends communicate and share in the good times and the bad. Friends talk to each other. In days gone by, we wrote letters and made phone calls. Today with the advent of the computer and e-mail capability, it is much easier and cheaper to communicate, especially if you are using the computer for other things. You are able to communicate in writing as if you were talking on the phone. So today we have been provided another communication tool that enables us to have interaction with our friends and family. In the "good old days," if our friends were not located nearby, communication was not as easy as today.

Friendship Maintenance

To me there are many types of friendship that we encounter at different times in the life cycle. When we were children we may have had a number of friends who were our playmates, but even then there was always one or two who were special. This year I had a pleasant surprise in that a former playmate and friend of some 60 years ago called me. He did not address me as Charles but as Herbert, which I had not heard in many years. I was amazed. Since that call we have started communicating again and plan to meet in the small town where we went to school and played together. I am sure that my wife will enjoy listening to his telling tall tales about me as a young boy. A nice old-fashioned country luncheon with my wife and long lost friend at the local cafe will be totally enjoyable. I believe it is important to capture memories on film, so I will definitely have my digital camera with me to capture this memory.

For most of us, our relationships with school friends are just a memory. Even in school there are categories of friends—friends that we have socially and sometimes those who are in school organizations such as cheerleading, school newspaper, drama club and sports. These organizations provide a bonding, due to the members having a common objective to reach a goal. Some people maintain these friendships throughout their lives. This is terrific, as you have the ability to mature together as friends and derive all the benefits that friends have to offer.

Another source of friendship is found among members of the armed services and veterans. Sharing their military service experiences together sometimes creates friendships for life, as evidenced by veteran reunions, American legion, and Veterans of Foreign Wars organizations.

Then there are the friendships that we develop in the workplace that are lasting as well. I know that we all have our work friends and, even in retirement, we get together as a group or individually.

Maybe we play some golf or the families get together and have lunch or take a ride to see the countryside. And as we mature and sometimes are limited in our activities, just a simple phone call or letter is a wonderful way to keep in touch. It's always a delight to hear a friend's voice and catch up on what is happening in your friend's life currently, as well as talk about the "good old days."

Friendships sometimes are of a short duration, as God brings different ones across our paths for different purposes. Then there are the "forever friends," who, though separated by time and distance, we can count on to be there for us in times of crisis. Whether short-term or long-term, we are blessed to have known and experienced true friendship.

We cannot choose the family into which we are born. Sometimes the family relationships are far from perfect and we can grow up without much feeling of belonging. However, we do get to choose our friends, and sometimes God uses those special people to take up the slack where our family members cannot or will not meet our needs.

At various times in our lives, we think back to past good times and the people who were a part of them. For some reason we have failed to tell them "thank you." This negligence usually is due to getting caught up in raising a family and all of the day-to-day living. Before you know it a decade or, in some cases, decades have passed. During this period we occasionally think of these people and decide to write or make a phone call just to say, "Hi." But again something happens and those thoughts disappear into the historical memory bank.

After my good experience of meeting with my old school friend, I decided to take the initiative and start looking up some of my other old friends. What a journey it has been! One is in Virginia, another in Arizona, another in New Mexico, and the list goes on and on. Surprisingly most have e-mail, but that is understandable because most were former "techies," as we say in the technology arena. They too were pioneers in the profession, as was I. We shared experiences about working seven days a week with twelve-hour days and being successful in implementing computer systems in the early days of computers. These friendships were formed in early adulthood but had been dormant for some thirty years. It was easy to revive these friendships because of the shared experiences. It was as if we just picked up where we left off. It was amazing to hear about their children and grandchildren and what course each had taken in life. They spoke with joy and were anxious to share their happiness. My only regret is that I did not make those phone calls sooner. Why? Because some of those friends who were my mentors have passed on to a "greater place" and I did not get the chance to say, "Thank you for being there for me."

* * * * *

Historical Moment from 1941
German aeronautical engineers have started to use
Konrad Zuse's Z3,
the world's first electronic computer.

* * * * *

Relationship Investments

Back in the forties, there was this young couple who were going to get married. Now the boy was a sailor and the girl was a beautiful black-haired green-eyed Irish girl. They both were poor in a materialistic sense but were rich in happiness and were going to get married in the church. The girl had a plain green suit, which she was going to get married in and this was okay. But there came a phone call from her aunt who had some years in the past had a huge church wedding and asked her niece if she would honor her by wearing her wedding dress. The niece, with a frog in her throat and tears in her eyes, said she would be honored. The wedding was complete due to that beautiful wedding dress and today they still have beautiful wedding pictures of that young man in a sailor's uniform and the beautiful black-haired green-eyed Irish girl in her flowing white wedding gown. Some time ago, the niece wrote her aunt a long letter thanking her once again for her gift of letting her wear her wedding dress and, most importantly, of her love that she had showed in one of the most special moments in her young life. They both were truly blessed again by giving a rebirth to a happy moment. This is a good example of how we can, in big and small ways, invest ourselves in others' lives. Is there someone in your past that you need to express appreciation?

Let's Do Lunch

As seniors we do value those relationships in the past that have enriched our lives and we are still actively forming friendships. Today we live in a fast-paced society, so we must take advantage of these opportunities whenever we can. The words "let's do lunch" have become a very important part of my senior life and I suspect many other seniors. I think this is the so-called "in" phrase (that I have borrowed) of business people today. Often they do not have time in a brief encounter to discuss business, so rather than push it aside, the code words "Let's do lunch" are used to set up a business meeting.

Now back in the good old days we had time or at least took the time to have a scheduled business dialogue, so we did not have to set up a meeting under the guise of a lunch break. At lunch time, we did what was expected—we ate lunch! Now there were exceptions when there were planned business luncheons, usually including people from other divisions or companies, with the purpose of creating a friendly atmosphere to discuss business. And then there were people who would barge into your office, come up to your table while your were having lunch or stop you in the hallway and start a conversation. Very tactfully it was said to the intruder, "Give me a call and we will set up a meeting to discuss..." rather than "I will call you next week and we will do lunch."

Back in the good old days we were not electronically wired with cell phones, pagers and other communication devices while we were out of the office having lunch or taking care of other personal matters. However, conducting business these days requires all kinds of electronic wizardry. For the young business person of today who is reading this book, I think it is great that you enjoy this dynamic environment. I must confess, however, based on my most recent experiences in the business world, I most definitely prefer the days of not being wired and taking the time that the company gave me to have lunch. I do not want to be available "24/7" (another current buzz word indicating you're never really off work). To me this has necessitated the need to use the phrase, "I will call you next week and we will do lunch."

So, the senior set has adopted this popular business phrase and given it a new meaning. These days the phrase, "Let's do lunch," means meeting with a friend(s) to enjoy each other's company without a business agenda. On numerous occasions when I have spoken, I have observed other seniors during lunch. Many times it is easy to observe because we seniors have a tendency to speak rather loudly. The conversations range from wartime experiences to grandchildren to significant business experiences. I totally enjoy these luncheons, as it is great to visit and reminisce of happenings gone by. We all talk a lot but we also are good listeners in that we really care to hear the news, regardless of the subject matter. Why? Because we are there because we want to be there—"doing lunch."

These are but a few small examples of reaching out again to those who were part of your lives and, for whatever reason, there has not been any communication for some period of time. I hope that you will stir up your own old memories and do something about contacting friends of long ago.

Chapter Six

Society

E ven as we think of days gone by, the memorable family moments and special friends, we can begin to get a concept of the stream of society over the years. If we look back far enough, we can see where we fit into the "scheme of things," as they say. We come to appreciate those whose lives impacted on us in positive ways and we also come to realize how our lives impact on others. The investments we have made in others ultimately will help shape what our society is becoming. To whom are the young listening? Are our voices as older Americans being heard? Do we still have the opportunity to influence others? Well, for one thing, our numbers are growing, as population statistics from the Encyclopedia Brittanica indicate:

> The United States is becoming a nation of adults, with an increasing proportion of its people in the middle- and upper-age brackets. The number of retired people has been increasing at a faster rate than the number of so-called productive workers (aged 18 to 64) and will increase still faster when the baby boom generation—people born between 1946 and 1964—reaches a normal retirement age after 2010.[33]

Let's take a moment and compare our society today with what it was a hundred years ago. How things have changed! These changes affect everything in our lives, including job wages, who is the breadwinner in the typical family, length of work week, economics, policies and regulations, etc. These are some areas of great change, as I see it. Some of these areas of change are:

- Education

Only 6 % of all Americans had graduated from high school in 1902. From the Encyclopedia Brittanica, we learn that:

> Before the 20th century [few new ideas of education] had caused little more than rumblings beneath the floor of the traditional schoolhouse. Because of John Dewey (1859–1952) they gathered force, and in the 1920s and 1930s new and old ideas collided right in the middle of the classroom.

> Some of the schools where neat rows of subdued children had sat immobilized in their bolted-down seats—listening to a teacher armed with textbook, lesson plan, grade book, and disciplinary ruler—became buzzing places where virtually everything moved, including the chairs. The children were occupied in groups or worked by themselves, depending on what they were doing. Above all, they were always doing: reading a favorite book, writing, painting, or learning botany by tending, observing, and discussing the plants they were growing. The teacher moved around the room, asking and answering questions, giving a child the spelling of a word he wanted to write or the pronunciation of a word he wanted to read, and in general acting as a helpful guide for the children's chosen activities. The chattering and noise and activity were signs that the children were excited about and absorbed by what they were doing. They were, in fact, learning by doing.[43]

You can see how education has evolved into something

very different from our methods of a century ago. Not only the methods have changed, the participants have as well. Even in the '30s and '40s, I remember children whose priorities were work over schooling. I had an uncle who had to stay after school as a disciplinary action but refused to stay, fearing his grandfather's giving him a whipping because he had work to do before the sun set for that day. Yes, back in the "good old days," whipping was used as a motivator to obey your parents.

To me, education really became available to the masses after World War II with the advent of the GI Bill. I personally not only utilized the GI Bill for my education but I purchased my first home that cost $11,400—WOW! This truly was a blessing, especially with our four little ones. I am sure that some of you can relate to this.

An amazing statistic from 1902 was that only one in ten adults could read and write. But this is understandable as these were still the pioneer days. The poor were busy working to make a living, working in sweatshops in the city or working the earth in the rural communities. In the '30s and '40s, we had a forty-eight hour work-week, which made it difficult to pursue continued education. Today, though, we have so many types of educational institutions with unlimited opportunities to be educated in a chosen career path.

- Birthplace

In 1902, more than 95 percent of all births in the United States took place in the home. Even in the '30s and '40s, this was common. I know that both of my grandmothers delivered their children at home and two of my aunts had their children at home. I was delivered at home by a doctor who was so old that he directed my father on how to introduce this child to life. So times have really changed. Today I don't hear the term "mid-wife," the one woman in the family who was an expert in delivering babies. In the old days, the families were much larger, as compared to today's typical family. The change from a rural farm community to the Industrial Age society has influenced many areas of our lives. Hospitals have replaced home births (although many hospitals offer "birthing rooms" now—what a novel idea!), and we can be thankful for the medical care available to us.

• Economy

How different the economy was a hundred years ago. This was a time when farms produced most of the food for families, while other needs such as sugar were bought at the general store in town for four cents a pound, eggs for fourteen cents a dozen, coffee for fifteen cents a pound. The cost of things is relative, of course, for the average worker only made between $200 and $400 per year. Now remember, we are talking about 1902.

Compared to today that sum certainly seems paltry. Our teenagers can make more than that today with part-time jobs flipping hamburgers. Remember, the government-imposed minimum wage was not set until later in history, and was enhanced by President Truman early in his administration.

In one hundred years in this country we have seen the economy rise to the heights of the Roaring Twenties and prosperous forties and fifties to the depths of the Great Depression and numerous times of recession. Many people today are afraid to invest, having seen their savings blown on a shaky economy. We are a society that depends on the Stock Market and "economic experts" and the government for our economic security. Maybe it is time to hearken back to the days when folks depended on God to provide for them (through hard work on their part), and appreciated that their basic needs were being met. They had a contentment that didn't depend on the ups and downs of the marketplace. Perhaps we need to emulate those of our forefathers who learned how to live without certain things and did not demand instant gratification. We are a consumer society, and I think there is far too much "consuming" going on. Let us not think so much of what we can get but rather what we can give to make our nation a better place to live.

• Communication

In 1902, a three-minute telephone call from Denver to New York City cost $11, and only 8% of the homes had telephones. What a difference a 100 years makes! And as I remember, the phone in the late thirties was on the wall and you reached the person that you were calling by the turning of a crank on the side of the phone. This would create the number of rings that the receiver would recognize as his own signal of an incoming call. Another thing about it—you could pick up the phone (even if you had not been called) and listen in to what your neighbors were talking about. This was the early version of what today's corporate world calls "teleconferencing." Excuse me for just a little humor.

* * * * *

Historical Moment from 1956
New phone lines cross Atlantic. The first transoceanic
telephone cable was completed this year, using two cables,
one for each direction.
* * * * *

Today we have telephone services "out of this world," but in addition, we can take our phones with us wherever we go, such as the theater, grocery stores, airplanes, and an infinite number of places. It has gotten to the point now that certain states are prohibiting the use of cell phones while driving, due to the allegation that talking on the phone can cause highway accidents. Theaters and other public places prohibit the use of cell phones, as well as certain time periods on airplanes and in certain areas of hospitals. Maybe we should take the hint that we do not really need to be as tied to this marvel as we think we do.

• Transportation
In 1902, there were only 8,000 cars in the country and only 144 miles of paved road. The speed limit in most cities was ten miles an hour. In the '30s, out in the country, there was no speed limit that I knew of because the cars could not go that fast. The one paved road that I was aware of was the famous Route 66, as all the side roads (country roads or spurs) were either dirt or gravel. I have several memories of when a farmer would "hitch" his horse to a Model A or T Ford to pull it out of the mud. I also remember being in a

wagon "going to town." We would drive the drivers of cars crazy, as we would be holding up traffic. We just thought those "city folks" were always in a hurry. When we went to town, which was very seldom, we rode in a wagon pulled by a team of horses. I remember being on the highway with cars following us trying to pass. Going to town was an all day event, as we purchased all the "store bought" items that we needed and you got caught up on the latest news. Now as far as automobiles are concerned, I knew only a few who could afford them. My friends and I had used cars and we all knew someone in the neighborhood who could fix them for us. But for those who could afford new cars they had a concern, which was expressed as, "Have you seen the new cars coming out next year? It won't be long before $5000 will only buy a used one." All things are relative, right?

We surely have come a long way in how we are able to move around in this day and age. I remember the Model A and T Fords. Did you know that Mr. Ford used the wood from the boxes that he got his parts in to provide the "running boards," used on cars to make it much easier to get into the vehicle? What an entrepreneur! Living on the farm, our main mode of transportation was called *walking*. You always hear the stories by the mature citizens saying, "In my day I walked two miles (or some amount of distance) to and from school every day." Well, I didn't walk that far but I know a lot of children that did walk many miles to school each day, carrying their "lunch pails." In addition, they had chores before and after school each day.

City transportation was mostly comprised of streetcars, buses, and service cars. Living in the city and going to high school in Clayton, Missouri meant riding the Easton streetcar to the Wellston Loop, then transferring to the city limits streetcar. It was quite an adventure for this country boy who was used to riding in a wagon or sometimes horseback out to work in the fields, or walking. When the weather was bad due to snow or ice, we hitchhiked, and that was acceptable and safe in those days.

We bought our "bus passes" each week in order to ride public service at a discount. We also had tokens that we could buy and we would have to get transfers to other lines in order to get to our final destination, if we were paying with coin for the ride.

The mode of transportation for the average person to travel across our great nation was predominately by bus or train. From St. Louis to Seattle was a three-day trip, as I remember, but what a delight! We were able to dine and have a fine meal while watching the beautiful scenery this country has to provide. Being able to sleep was a challenge but the young hardly noticed. This was not a high-speed train, which was fine with me because I could really take in the landscape passing by my window.

Streetcars for the most part are now transportation museum pieces. We still have the buses but not as many lines and not as frequent. I would not like to depend on getting to work in South County while living in North County, which I am sure some people must do in order to work at certain companies.

Airlines are the main mode of transportation for business as well as pleasure destinations. We are talking about hours now rather than days. This is good if you need to get some place fast, which is the way we live today, but if you want to take that train, you still can. It is a lot faster, so look real fast as you go by that lovely landscape that this great country provides. I have traveled all over these United States and I still say that in my opinion, Missouri is the most beautiful state of them all, whether it is seen from a wagon pulled by a team of horses or driving in one of today's fast cars.

America's love affair with the automobile began early in the twentieth century, but I must say that today, it's less like a love affair than it is like an unhealthy addiction. According to the Encyclopedia Brittanica, the number of cars, vans, trucks, and buses in the world now averages at least one for every 12 human beings…[and there are]…approximately 165 million registered automotive vehicles in the United States.[54] While the US led the world in car production through the 1980s, it has now given up its position to Japan, the world's largest producer. Can you imagine how that many cars in the world affect our environment? We now think we cannot live without our automobiles, as we enjoy the freedom to travel, whether it be across town or across the country. Yes, we are spoiled on our independence, but we need to be responsible citizens in protecting our environment. When cars first became available, it was not uncommon for people in a buggy pulled by a horse to come upon drivers who were stranded on the side of the road with car trouble. The prevailing advice was, "Next time, take your horse!" Maybe there is some wisdom in this anecdote—not that we should return to horse and buggy days, but perhaps we should walk more and drive less. Remember when we thought nothing of walking to the store that was a mile or two away? Well, we didn't have any trouble burning off those calories, did we? Now we try to get the closest possible parking space at the mall or business we are visiting so that we don't have to walk very far. It is true we have made great progress in modes of transportation, but let us not forget about those God-given means of transportation called feet! Let us enjoy what we have, but at the same time, take time to appreciate the slower pace of life that we experienced "way back when" when life was not speeding past us on the freeway. You might say that the twentieth century trotted in on horse and buggy and zoomed out on the space shuttle. Who would've thought?

* * * * *

Historical Tidbit from 1927
Motoring in the US will soon become easier as a
result of the introduction of the same type of
road signs across the country.

* * * * *

- Healthcare

The five leading causes of death in the United States in 1902 were pneumonia and influenza, tuberculosis, diarrhea, heart disease, and finally, stroke. There has been tremendous progress in the medical field in the elimination of these causes of death but unfortunately we have some new ones that have taken their place. We now have HIV, many types of cancer, diabetes, and the still prevalent heart disease. It is my opinion (though I do not claim to be a medical expert) that in the past we had many deaths that could have been attributed to diabetes, cancer and some of the diseases that we recognize today, but at that time they were not recognized. But also it is my belief that a lot of the diseases of today such as HIV are caused by a loss of morality and high-risk behavior. "You reap what you sow."

* * * * *

Historical Moment from 1942
Major quantities of penicillin are being produced.
It is hoped that the wonder cure may soon be available
for mass miracles on the battlefield.

* * * * *

Time continues to march on and with that we as a society will continue to progress relative to technology, medicine and the sciences. In conjunction with this progress the one thing that we must maintain and continue to improve upon is the morality of our nation. It is my firm belief that all of the advances that we achieve will be meaningless and will be subject to destruction if high standards of morality and integrity are not maintained.

We should not be amazed at these differences because the world has changed and will continue to change, whether it is economics, demographics, politics, or social issues. One thing that remains the same is human life. This being said, I pray that we as human beings will be consistent in maintaining the highest of standards as it relates to morality, love for one another and, most importantly, integrity.

CHAPTER SEVEN

A Potpourri of Opinions on Public Life

Having compared what our nation was like in the early twentieth century with how things are now, I think it is worth considering how our freedoms have eroded and how we ourselves have been taken captive by the wrong thinking of many in our society. When we read the news about such things as obese people suing restaurants for making them fat, or dependence on government to make laws concerning every conceivable action, we stand back and think, "What ever happened to common sense?"

Common Sense in Eating

We as members of this free society who are blessed to live in this country must continue to maintain our freedoms, such as the freedom to worship, to vote, freedom of speech, freedom of religion, freedom of choice, etc. These freedoms mean that government cannot interfere with our lives in these areas. Unfortunately for many, it is government from which we need to be freed.

It is my opinion that lately our freedoms are being threatened little by little. My concern is that this may be a continuing trend, which challenges not only our basic freedoms, but encroaches upon other choices we make, including such things as what we eat. There has been no action as of this writing to create laws that would impact our freedom of choice as to what we eat, but there is discussion in the media that perhaps restaurants should be more regulated so that they will offer only food that is considered healthy. When I was young, I didn't need any other guide than my grandmother, whose philosophy was expressed in statements like, "Clean your plate because of the starving people in China." I know the underlying principle behind her admonition was that we should be appreciative of what we have because many do without. Of course this was "slow food," with mostly healthy choices on the menu. Our idea of "fast food" was what people ate at Lent. Today, it appears that everybody is in a hurry. Many don't take the time to come home and enjoy the whole family's sitting down to hot home-cooked meals and discussing the day's happenings by all members of the family. There is a lot more to healthy eating than just the food one chooses to eat. Maybe we wouldn't have so many problems with obesity if we changed the environment in which we eat. Think about that. I guess Grandma was ahead of her time—what a nutritionist!

The concern about restaurant food is raised because of the problem of obesity in children. There is no denying the fact that our young people (and older as well) are becoming obese. If you doubt this, just notice the wedding announcement page in your local newspaper (check out the brides' pictures) or go "people-watching" at the mall, or you might want to look in the mirror. But do we really need government to regulate what we eat? Again, I say, "What ever happened to common sense?"

I know there is value in people's protesting a certain practice in public life, and much good can come from this. For instance, many of the major fast food chains have changed the way they fry foods, using healthier alternatives to lard (which was the standard for many years). They have done this as a result of the public outcry and have not needed government interference to make the necessary changes.

I am a firm believer that if you want to eat fast foods, that is your choice, and the thought of anyone's tampering with this choice gives me great concern. There is one word that I feel is relative to the things that we do in life and that word is **moderation**. I believe we can over-exercise. I believe that we can consume too much alcohol and lose our sense of reasoning. I believe we can overwork and overeat and the list goes on and on. So if you eat certain fast foods three meals a day and seven days a week, you may develop a health problem. You have that choice. If you are a parent, you are responsible to provide direction in the kinds of choices that your children make. You can and should teach them to eat "healthy" from the time they are little babies until they leave the nest. I can remember my wife's always urging the children, "Eat your greens." I suspect that in this day and age when people are seeking someone to blame for their human frailties, that many parents are trying to avoid taking responsibility for bringing up their children to make healthy choices in life. In regards to suing the restaurants and blaming others for our bad behavior, I want to say emphatically that we are *not* a nation of victims. The decisions as to what we eat are ours to make, knowing that our choices have consequences.

Let's apply some more logic to the argument for government legislation in this area of our health. But first, just think about the fact that certain individuals are even discussing this as an issue. Why? I feel that my fellow citizens and I don't have to be told what to do to eat right. I solicit information from the health agencies and health experts as to what their opinions are relative to certain foods and food supplements, as they have done the research and have the expertise. Once I read or listen to this information, I feel I can make the conscious decision of whether or not to eat French fries three times a week with a chocolate malt with a cherry on top. I do not want the government telling the restaurants what they can cook and put on the menu, based on what may or may not be good for their customers. We are smart enough to stay away from food that may be harmful to us. However, remember, what we consider not to be good for us may be fine for someone else.

It seems that we are hearing more and more stories about what I call frivolous lawsuits like the case of the lady spilling coffee on her lap and burning herself, or some such nonsense. I know when I have a cup of coffee, I want it hot, and when I receive this coffee that I purchased to drink, it is my responsibility not to spill it on myself or burn myself. We do have responsibilities. By the way, I bet we all send our coffee back if it is cold. How about the logic of certain people who are getting ready to attack the food industry for making people obese? What's next? Will we attack the automobile industry because we get traffic tickets? Or maybe we can sue the same industry for making cars that go too fast? Think about that.

* * * * *

Historical Moment from 1948
The first McDonald's Restaurant (the Golden Arches)
opens in San Bernadino, California.

* * * * *

We Americans are very smart people and we are responsible for our well being. We need laws that protect our freedoms. We do not need laws that infringe on our choices concerning what we eat. Now it is a given, if there is something found in our food that will kill us due to its being poisonous, we need the government to step in. We need the government inspectors to inspect those meat-packing houses and other food processing companies to assure safety in what we eat. This is great, but I don't want anyone to tell me that I cannot eat broccoli or a French fry occasionally. Let the companies determine the products they offer to the consumer, using sensible guidelines concerning preparation. You note I said "offer," but the choice of whether or not to order it should be ours, based on whether or not we think it is okay to eat it. I must share with you that for the last thirty years I have followed a strict diabetic diet. Basically, the desire to have a long healthy life prompted my strict adherence to this diet. Simply, *I* chose, not the government, nor my doctor, nor even my wife—to eat the foods that were "right" for me. I say, "Government, stay out of my kitchen as you have more important matters on your plate, such as terrorism, protecting our freedoms, etc."

More Common Sense

There are other matters concerning what may be good for us

that require common sense. Let's do a little more comparing between "then and now."

• Smoking

There was a time when smoking cigarettes, cigars and pipes was commonplace. I even remember doctors doing cigarette commercials on television and our favorite actors were portrayed with the "sophisticated" cigarette in their hands. There was also the "Marlboro Man," which of course all full-blooded young macho men wanted to emulate. For some of the stronger of heart, a good chaw of "Red Man" was what you needed to quench that thirst. The concern in years gone by was that cigarettes may go up to a quarter a pack, prompting smokers to say, "I am going to quit." Today, based on research, most citizens have awakened to the fact that smoking can cause cancer and can kill you. So, smoker, back in the "old days," there were no crusades to stop smoking but just the opposite.

The gist of this little message is (as in making healthy choices), I believe you should make healthy choices about that to which you subject yourself. It is not the campaigners or the government that is going to suffer the consequences for your smoking—you are. Even though many of my day from the '30s, '40s, and '50s made unwise choices in this area, I think many of those choices were made in ignorance of the consequences of this "habit," and unfortunately, many of our number have succumbed to diseases caused by tobacco. There really is no excuse today—we are a well-informed society. It's sort of like whether or not to choose to "super-size" that hamburger or whatever. You know the effects of unwise choices, whether it is unhealthy eating or smoking, drinking, or doing drugs. Wise up!

* * * * *

Historical Moment from 1954
February 12 – A US study links cancer with smoking.

* * * * *

- Language

Another area of concern in public life is the coarsening of our language as a culture. Think about how foul language was viewed in the past. A parent might have said, "I'm afraid to send my kids to the movies anymore. Ever since they let Clark Gable get by with saying 'damn' in 'Gone With The Wind,' it seems every new movie has either 'hell' or 'damn' in it." How about the views concerning nudity on the screen? Remember when in the movie, " It Happen One Night," Clark Gable took his shirt off and he did not have on an undershirt? This caused an uproar! (It might be noted that undershirt sales went down as all the men wanted to be like Mr. Gable.) Boy, we sure have come a long way! It seems that these days nothing shocks us. As a society, we have become hardened to violence, desensitized to crude and profane language, and unashamed of shameful acts—all in living color and bigger than life—on the silver screen.

- The Mail

Among my senior friends and acquaintances, I often hear complaints about the cost of postage. Now I do not own a business so I do not know the impact of today's postal costs relative to the company's "bottom line," but as a private citizen, paying thirty-seven cents to mail a letter is, in my opinion, a real bargain. We have the best postal service in the world and we get our money's worth. For those who have experienced mailing letters out of the Continental USA, I am sure you can tell some "war stories." The concern "back when" was, "Did you hear the post office is thinking about charging a dime just to mail a letter?" I still say that thirty-seven cents is a bargain, considering the quality service that we are provided by our United States Postal Service. Incidentally, this is not a paid commercial—just an attempt to get things in perspective and realize once again the blessings we enjoy in America. With the advent of electronic mail, I wonder what the scenario will be like five to ten years from now—just a thought.

- Sports

Remember several decades ago, it was common to be discussing around the water cooler: "Hey! Did you hear where some baseball player just signed a contract for $75,000 a year just to play ball? It wouldn't surprise me if someday they'll be making more than some of our leaders of industry." Well, today there are a lot of baseball players making more than leaders of industry. However, these same leaders have life-time benefits that I am guessing are much greater than the ball players have. This is another case of how economics have changed and will continue to change from "way back when."

- Electricity

"I never thought I'd see the day all our kitchen appliances would be electric. They are even making electric typewriters now." This would have been a comment back in the fifties and sixties. Oh, how far we've come! You know, I don't think we have typewriters in offices anymore today. Now I do remember seeing one in a back office of a firm that occasionally used it to type an exceptional label for a package. Today, personal computers have replaced typewriters, making just one more work tool a museum piece. As for as appliances in kitchens, they are all-electric, right down to the can openers. At my house, we do have an old fashioned opener for when we go on vacations or in case of power blackout, but I suspect many of the younger generation don't even know what one looks like. In some homes, when you walk into the room at night, the lights automatically go on and if you want to turn on the television, just clap your hands. It's probably not a good idea to start clapping your hands during a program, though, as you might really confuse your television.

Well, I know that this section includes a rather eclectic collection of items to help us compare "then" and "now," and I might be giving the impression that I think everything about the "good ole' days" was good. Some might even accuse me of living in the past.

However, I think there is value in reflecting on the changes in our society. We refer to things in the past regardless if they were better or worse than today. In the area of values, we have to say things are worse now, but in relation to medical care, scientific advancements and the comforts we enjoy today, we have to say we are better off. So let us enjoy our retelling of the stories of the past, and maybe in the hearing of them, someone (or perhaps many) will reflect on those values that we hold dear as well.

This Is Progress?

It is true we have made progress in many ways that have been for the betterment of society. We have made great advances in terms of material success, but I think perhaps this has also contributed to our downfall as a culture. Extreme materialism as we have it today has led to extreme excess in many areas. What are some of these areas?

- Drinking

Did you ever think that maybe, just maybe, we as a society drink too much? Can this be attributed to living in the "fast lane," socializing with the boss to try and climb the corporate ladder? (Just a thought—the fast lane often is littered with the wreckage of reckless drivers.) Some colleges and universities have been given ratings as to which ones have the best parties. Now think about that! Shouldn't the objectives of higher education be to prepare young people to enter the work force? Instead, the kind of students who just want to party end up being a liability to society. Yes, our society has a problem not only with smoking but addiction to alcohol. It is my opinion that having a drink now and then is not a problem but, as always, in life we should do everything in moderation. It is true that we had drinking problems back in the good old days, but it is my belief that it was not as prevalent as today. And why is that? Our culture has changed to a fast-paced environment, resulting in the decline in our social values. And they call this progress?

- Driving

Do we drive too fast? You bet we do! I really think that we have now a generation of kamikaze drivers on the highways (for the younger folks' information: kamikaze pilots were Japanese who made suicide missions in World War II). I am amazed how these large trucks are driving at 70 to 80 miles an hour in a 60 mile-an-hour zone. If there is a pouring rain and one of those giant sixteen wheelers go past, creating a wind vacuum and a large amount of spray over surrounding cars, it gives us opportunity to increase our prayer life. Of course, praying might not be a bad thing to do when you're on the highway—just pray with your eyes open!

We also have to watch out for the people who run red lights, the drag racers and the drivers who weave in and out of traffic at high speeds. How about people on the freeway at 4:30 PM who get into the right lane to pass cars already in line going straight and then try to jump in front of those in line? This causes us to struggle to maintain our composure. This kind of driver (of course it's always the "other driver") reveals his character with his driving habits. One can say we have made progress in the building of automobiles but in the process we have lost the courtesy of the road.

- Treatment of others

In listening to the news and reading the papers, I have come to the conclusion that today we hate too much and love too seldom our fellow human beings. This is true in the Middle East, Korea, and the War on Terrorism, but on a smaller scale, among our own politicians. The kind of "one-upmanship" we see in the mud-slinging campaigns of politics makes me sick These are adults who act like little kids. We must ask the question—are we really making progress in this world?

These are just a few of the areas in which I think we digress rather than progress. What can we do about it? How can we turn the tide? Well, we can pray a little more, we can be role models of what we profess, and we can teach the younger generation of the good in maintaining a high standard of social values. We must do this if we want to continue as a loving human race. It is my firm belief that in order to maintain the freedoms upon which this country was founded, we must maintain those values which were foundational in the creation of the Declaration of Independence and the Bill of Rights. So help us, God.

- Crime

Crime today is so prevalent that we keep statistics on the categories of crime such as murder and rape. We now have a war on drugs. We now have metal detectors in schools and our children have to wear identification tags. As I write this article, a youth of 14 years is alleged to have shot the principle of his Jr. High School and then in turn killed himself. This happened in York County in Pennsylvania. It is not uncommon to hear of a killing in school. It is not uncommon to hear in the news of a spouse killing his/her mate and in some cases the children. We hear about our sports figures that are involved in some type of crime.

Now we have corporate crime where top executives are "fixing the books" to show earnings that are not real and they are being discovered. This, in turn, impacts our economy and the everyday folks who are trying to make a living. This is just another factor that contributes to the loss of confidence in the stock market and in turn a lot of retirement accounts, that are heavily invested into stocks, causing the investor to take a tremendous hit. And if you are a retiree dependent on that account to draw your monthly check, it is horrific, as seniors do not have time to re-enter the work force and build another "retirement nest." Now with the prevalence of this type of "white collar crime" in our society, it has become just another way in which the values of integrity and honesty are being eroded. When this white-collar crime was found out to be so extensive, it was all over the news. We don't hear too much about it anymore but there are other corporations who are being investigated about their accounting practices. Typically, the media does not give it much attention after awhile. I wonder how many chief executives responsible for these crimes against a retiree's retirement fund are currently doing jail time. Is this another way in which we have become desensitized?

Not only can we point an accusing finger at those in "big business" who are ripping us off without conscience, we must also acknowledge that there is a desensitization toward "petty crimes." I can remember the day when a person got a traffic ticket, it was a big deal. It was not only costly but also embarrassing and it was something we did not talk about. We were very sensitive about this. Not so today, with the proliferation of "radar detectors" and "attitude" toward the laws and those who enforce them.

Everyday Folks

One of the beauties of our political system in America is that each individual counts, regardless of social status, wealth, or position. Looking to the past, we readily acknowledge that many of our forebears have been ordinary people who established a government which is "for the people" and "by the people." We might call them "just everyday folks." Today, these are the average citizens that make our nation great. Why am I writing about everyday folks? Because we sometimes feel that we as individuals don't count, and this is so far from the truth. I can't add up the number of times that I have heard, "What can I do about it?" regarding all aspects of life from politics to taxes.

As I remember, back in the good old days, most of my family's business transactions were with everyday folks, dealing with the corner family grocery, the barber shop, the family owned drugstore (with soda fountains), the family doctor (who made house calls), and the neighborhood car repair shop. This environment has changed dramatically, particularly in the cities. Now we have the large impersonal grocery store chains, drugstores and so forth. I am not saying this is bad but I do miss those personal relationships that we had with the everyday business folk, which gave us the feeling that we had more of a voice in the community.

* * * * *

Historical Tidbit from the 20th Century
By 2000, almost half of the world's population lived in cities.
This has led to more joblessness and poverty, as well as crime
and the breakdown of the nuclear family.

* * * * *

Let's not forget that the everyday folks have been our heroes in wars from Rosie the Riveter to GI Joe, securing those freedoms that we hold dear. We as everyday folks can be heroes as well when we go to the polls and voice our votes. Even a few votes can make the difference in an election. A recent presidential election (2000) that focused on Florida's voters is a case in point. The main focus came down to the point of hundreds of votes that would determine the outcome of the Florida electoral vote. There were some local elections throughout the country that came down to several votes that separated the winners from the losers. So we the average folks do count.

There are many average people who, with a common objective, have formed

organizations in order to have a powerful voice in matters from Medicare to taxes. These kinds of organizations not only help in terms of national issues, but local ones as well. So maybe if you want to voice your opinions but feel that you as an individual do not have the clout, maybe you should join the appropriate organization and become an active member.

On a lighter note, there are some "just for fun" organizations as well. In America today, it seems there is a support group or organization of some kind for every imaginable activity. One such organization we seniors can enjoy is the local dance club. For most of us, this would be what's considered ballroom dancing—not necessarily limited to the sedate waltz. Many of us want to get out there and "boogie"—we who love the music of the 40s and 50s. Well! With the dance clubs you as an average person can now boogie all night if you want to.

In the work world, the everyday folks who own the small businesses are the backbone of this country's economy. They are the entrepreneurs who invest their monies, time, creativity and faith in their ability to make it happen. They are the employers who create the jobs. I take my hat off to these people as they have the "guts" to put everything on the line. I know of an individual who started his company and was down to the brink of failure with only a few thousand dollars in the bank. This one morning he broke down in tears because he had a family with small children and was the sole provider. His business future looked extremely gloomy. But that same day he got a big contract for his product and his company was saved. Today this company is a multi-million dollar organization providing employment for everyday folks who are making an above average wage. They have been with this entrepreneur throughout the bad times and the good times alike. Success comes when ordinary people team up and share the goals of their leaders. Again, we should applaud them for their contribution to the good life we enjoy.

What we must do, even if we feel that we are the only ones with a specific viewpoint, and there is no specific organization already formed that expresses that viewpoint, we can contact people who are responsible for making things happen and let them know what we think. This can be as simple as writing a letter to the editor of your local newspaper. Let your voice be heard and our country will be a better place because of it, even if you are just "everyday folk."

Among the everyday folk of my childhood and early adulthood were the people down at the old barbershop in town. When I would go in to get my "traditional" haircut, I would often hear: "Hi, Cleve! Hi, Mack! Hi, Charles!" These were just a few of the familiar friends at the shop who went there for more than one reason. The personal touch (friendliness, being called by name) was just as important as the haircut style. My layman's definition of a traditional haircut is the use of a razor on the neck, around the ears, trimming of eyebrows and the ears and, in my case, the trimming of my beard. It's amazing how hair grows in all of the wrong places as you get older and how it starts to disappear where it is supposed to be. As I sat in the barbershop waiting for my turn to get into the barber's chair, my thoughts drifted to times past.

When I was a boy, I had a front row seat in my position of "shoeshine boy," so I could watch the activities that went on in the barbershop. To make some spending money I shined shoes on Saturdays. I got ten cents a shine and when I got a tip I was in "Hog Heaven." In order for me to have the privilege of working in the shop, I had the following duties. I swept up the hair during the day and at the end of the day. I made sure the magazines and papers were stacked nicely and neatly and were the current issues. When the gentlemen were finished with their haircuts, I used a clothes brush to brush their backs to make sure there was no hair on their clothes. Opening the door for them, I stated, "Come back again, sir." I also performed other duties as the barbers dictated. Again, I considered myself as being blessed to have this opportunity to make my own money.

The barbershop was the gathering place for conversations and, in the days of my boyhood, those conversations were concerning the war and its impact. Men talked about their relatives in the service, and guessing what theater of war they were in. They had to guess due to government secrecy. Another topic of conversation was how individuals were coping with rationing.

The barber, in my opinion, was the listener and a person of true understanding, much as a chaplain would be. He did not provide specific remedies but provided the listening ear. It was a place where the customer would just talk, and in retrospect, I feel it provided him an outlet to get things off of his chest. This service was just a part of the barber's job, with no extra charge to the customer. Today we term this as multi-tasking.

The barbershop was the place to post your cards for the turkey shoot and Boy Scout and Girl Scout drives. Schools would ask permission to put their ads in the window. It was one of the small town's centers of communication and in the large cities, it was the neighborhood center of communication.

I was also always amazed at the memories the barbers had. They knew all of the athletes on the high school teams. They remembered my name and how I wanted to have my hair cut.

In some ways, today's barbershop is much the same, except for the opportunity to get my shoes shined. However, it appears to me the traditional shop and barber is slowly disappearing. To me this is sad, as this is a part of the generation that so many of my readers grew up in starting in the 30s. So, for my young readers who have not experienced the "Old Time Barber Shop," if nothing more, give it a try so that you can add this to your memory bank as it relates to "then" and "now." A PS to this story is that in the '30s and '40s, I never met a barber who couldn't sing—hence, the origin of "The Barber Shop Quartet."

CHAPTER EIGHT

Values

I have said much about how our social values have eroded in the US. I suppose there are many reasons for this and I realize that we older folks are sometimes blamed for the ills of society. However, though we certainly can take the blame for some things, I want to stand up for my senior friends because, in spite of our faults, we did manage to uphold strong societal values through many traumatic changes in our nation's history. This is strictly from my perspective, keeping in mind that I consider myself in the "golden years" of my life. In this section, I would like to mention a few of the differences in thinking between the older generations and the younger ones. Some things are just personal preference, I know, but there are also underlying principles that need to be reflected upon.

- Immodesty and Inappropriate Dressing

Based on observation of today's culture, I would have to say that the pride of appearance must be almost non-existent. For example, today it is quite common to see people attending church wearing shorts and other types of vacation apparel. Did you ever notice the after church restaurant senior crowd? The ladies are so nicely and modestly dressed, with the finest of accessories, and hairdo in place. The men wear coats and ties. This scene to me is slowly disappearing. This is but one example about pride in appearance. I do not even want to go into what some people are doing to and adding to their bodies for the sake of so-called fashion. I wonder if the underlying principle here is the lack of pride in appearance shows a lack of self-worth. I think that would fit today's generation in many ways.

* * * * *

Historical Tidbit from 1939
Nylon stockings are now available, replacing the more delicate natural silk stockings. Nylon was discovered in 1937 by a chemist at the Du Pont Company, and it can also be used to make parachutes.

* * * * *

- Irreverence and Religion

One thing the older generation cannot be blamed for is kicking God out of school. We had prayer in the football locker room before the game or other activities. Public display of Christmas scenes was accepted without questioning. The displaying of the Ten Commandments in public places was also accepted. We were not afraid to use "religious" language in television and movies. I believe that our religious freedoms are being eroded as we see these "things of the past" being attacked. What next? The burning of churches? The Gestapo persecuting religious people again? It will be a sad day when these freedoms we hold dear are taken from us because of our acceptance of "that's just the way things are these days, and ain't it awful!"

- Misuse of Language

The older generations did not denigrate our English language. Sometime, just listen to the language you hear while taking a walk in the mall or while at work. Civilized and refined speech is also absent from much of the media, including movies, magazines, and tabloid newspapers, not to mention today's music. We are not only "dumbing down" our language, we are reflecting through our language the degradation of humankind. This is cause for concern and I for one hope that this is an area of public life that will be changed soon.

There is also a change in many of our common phrases from the past. Take, for example, words and phrases like: time-sharing; draft dodger; made in Japan; coke; pot; rock music. Here are some old definitions for those terms:

Time-sharing – meant time the family spent together in the evenings and on weekends, not purchasing of a condominium on the lake front property.

Draft dodger – was someone who closed the front door when the evening breeze started. If you were lucky enough to be by a window that was across from the door and there was an evening breeze while you slept…instant, free air-conditioning.

Made in Japan – Anything that had "Made in Japan" on it was considered to be junk. Now it is rare that we can find anything that says it was made in America. I feel that our country is headed to becoming a nation of services and that more and more of our manufactured goods will be imported.

Coke – a cold carbonated drink you got at the local drug-store soda fountain or out of a refrigerated box that had real glass bottles of Coca-colas hanging in a row of slots. You inserted your nickel, pushed a lever, and the bottle would be released. We enjoyed the stimulant but it didn't cause us to hallucinate or become addicted as in today's "coke" (cocaine) users.

Pot – was something that Mom cooked in and "grass" was something you mowed. How marijuana came to be called "pot" I don't know, but I can see the analogy involved in calling it "grass," as it is a plant.

Rock music – In the good old days (before the fifties), rock music was the lullaby Mom sang as she rocked the baby in that old-fashioned rocking chair. Today's rock music (played at extremely high volume) makes you feel like you've been hit by a rock in the head!

I guess we seniors are sometimes considered old-fashioned but, as for as I am concerned, I am proud to thought of in this way. I am not ashamed of what we considered in our day to be almost sacred. I love the meanings of words and phrases such as "one nation UNDER GOD" in the "Pledge of Allegiance to the Flag." In years gone by these were never questioned and it was a privilege and honor to serve our country as so many of our young people are doing today. Some in our society (and I think they are a small very vocal minority) challenge the very fundamental beliefs behind such words, but I believe in the end these objectors will not succeed.

* * * * *

Gotta Love that Judge!

In Florida, an atheist became incensed over the preparation for Easter and Passover holidays and decided to contact the local ACLU about the discrimination inflicted on atheists by the constant celebrations afforded to Christians and Jews with all their holidays while the atheists had no holiday to celebrate.

The ACLU jumped on the opportunity to once again pick up the cause of the godless and assigned their sharpest attorneys to the case.

The case was brought before a wise judge who after listening to the long, passionate presentation of the ACLU lawyers, promptly banged his gavel and declared, "Case dismissed!"

The lead ACLU lawyer immediately stood and objected to the ruling and said, "Your honor, how can you possibly dismiss this case? Surely the Christians have Christmas, Easter and many other observances. And the Jews—why in addition to Passover they have Yom Kippur and Hanukkah ...and yet my client and all other atheists have no such holiday!"

The judge leaned forward in his chair and simply said "Obviously your client is too confused to know about or for that matter even celebrate the atheists' holiday!"

The ACLU lawyer pompously said "We are aware of no such holiday for atheists, just when might that be, your honor?"

The judge said "Well it comes every year on exactly the same date—-April 1st!"

"The fool says in his heart, 'There is no God.'"
- Psalm 14:1, Psalm 53:1

HOORAY FOR THAT JUDGE!

(Unknown Author)

* * * * *

- Impolite Behavior

Those of us of the senior set did not destroy politeness and civility in our behavior. This is seen everyday: road rage; disregard for traffic laws; disrespect by burning the flag; disrespect shown to educators, law enforcement personnel and others in authority. It is sad to say, but the disrespect for mothers, fathers and other family members is rampant. This one really bothers me, as I have seen children at the age of nine telling their mother to "shut up." Children of my youth never even thought about giving any "back talk" to our family members or any adults. Ho we behaved was to bring honor, not shame, to the family name. Oh, that we could return to this value!

- Irresponsible Spending

Do we spend recklessly? In my opinion, our current society spends way too much on what is unneeded and unwise. This is evident in the increase of bankruptcy cases. Credit card debt is out of sight, and there seems to be no stopping people's tendency to become indebted "over their heads." It has become so bad that the government is now sticking their toes into the pond.

In the 30s, 40s and 50s, we did not spend money imprudently. Generally, there was one person who was bringing home a paycheck. In those days, we did not have courses entitled "Money Management" or companies that would help consolidate our debts. We just had what I call common sense when it came to money. Our main goal was to provide shelter for the family. We did not strive to have several cars(in most cases, we had no car), a vacation cruise, or a bigger house. Saving for a college education was nothing but a dream for most of us. We had our dreams, but they were, in my opinion, earthier and were more attainable financially. We lived within our means. I can't remember how many times I have heard when I was growing up, "You must live within your means." Sound familiar, my fellow seniors?

To me, I feel this matter of financial responsibility is very important to write about because it does have an impact on society as a whole. Historically, nations have crumbled because of their permissive societies. I am not the first or only person to write about this subject matter, nor will I be the last, but I wanted to get my "two cents worth" in to help the cause.

What About Today?

While it is easy to lament over the downward direction that our nation is going, I must say that the news is not all bad. I am seeing some signs that there are still those of the younger generation that respect the values of the older generation and honor them by following their examples. I would like to share with you some of my experiences that have served to encourage me in this area.

Recently, while attending a silent auction event at my grand-daughter's university, I sat back and watched her and her school-mates manage the auction. I thought, "how time flies," remembering her as a little girl and now seeing her in this leadership position that brought me great pride. I sat there in amazement while watching how my granddaughter and her friends ran this event. They were very organized and had developed a tremendous business process to make the event a success. The money raised from the auction was to be donated to a building project at the school. The total number of donations was above expectations. The attendees were the parents and grandparents of the students.

Also, it was really great to seeing the bonding of the students with several of the professors who were in attendance. As they were introduced the young ladies gave them a tremendous applause, which we could tell was sincere. So I do want to note the dedication of these representatives of higher education.

As I listened to my granddaughter give a short speech prior to the auction, my mind went back in time to when she was a little girl. Now that little girl is not more, but was standing in front of her parents, grandparents, fellow students and some of the faculty. She had blossomed into a young lady with intelligence, kindness and a person who shows love for her fellow human beings. It was not only her that showed these attributes but also her fellow classmates who demonstrated these qualities to total strangers. It was apparent only after a few minutes that we felt their human kindness.

Time has passed since seeing my granddaughter as a little girl going shopping with her mother and grandmother and those times that she stayed overnight with Grandma and Grandpa. I was blessed that I was given the occasional opportunities that I had to sit with her to review her homework when she was in grade school. It was especially meaningful for me to review her homework when the subject covered the era of World War II or economics as a high school student. Now I did not do the work but was a real live source of information about the social values of the '30s and '40s that those of us of the grandparent set held dear. What an opportunity!

Additionally, I would hear Grandma telling her things from the Bible as well as giving her religious articles. I remember many, many years ago when my own grandmother sat at the kitchen table and we read from the Bible by the light of a lamp. How time flies but we still have those wonderful memories.

This was an occasion that said to me there is hope in this world and just maybe we can regain the social values that we had back in the '30s and '40s. This challenge is on the shoulders of our young people of today and even though time seems to be flying faster and faster, as we seniors get older we still can be an influence on this younger generation whenever the opportunity presents itself. So we still have a duty to perform whether it is the opportunity to slip in a dialogue when we are reviewing homework or we're at a function in which we can tell them how proud we are of them.

So, adults of all ages, recognize that time is fleeting, and you need to take the time to teach and guide the younger members of the family on the importance of showing respect, being a person of integrity, showing compassion and the love for your fellow human being. It will provide you wonderful memories in later life and you will be able to say to yourself, "Thank you, God for letting me be an influence on their lives."

A good example of how we as seniors can encourage our young

people is the "Voice of America" program. Recently I had the extreme pleasure of participating as one of the judges to select the Missouri finalist in the Veterans of Foreign Wars (VFW) program entitled "The Voice of Democracy." This program is a National Audio/Essay Competition to allow ninth through twelfth grade high school students to voice their opinions on their responsibility to our nation. The program theme changes annually. The 2003-2004 theme is: "MY COMMITMENT TO AMERICA'S FUTURE."

When I was called upon to be one of three judges, I considered what an opportune time to listen to what some of these young people had to say relative to the theme. There were fifteen finalists representing their districts within the state of Missouri. It was refreshing to hear these youth, in that they were not like the portrayal of youth in the media.

The National Association of Broadcasters initiated the Voice of Democracy Program in 1946. Four winners were selected from the North, South, East and West regions of our country; each winner received a $500 savings bond and a wristwatch. The second year a gentleman by the name of Charles Kuralt was one of the winners. He later became an internationally known journalist. Other winners were Anita Bryant and John Ashcroft, also well-known in our country in the worlds of entertainment and politics. The VFW assumed sole responsibility for the program in 1961.

In 1964, the Ladies Auxiliary joined the VFW's sponsorship. As a result of the cooperation the VFW organization has received from many high school teachers across the nation, the participation from many high school students has been strong.

Just to show the growth of this VFW program, it has reached from a level of four national winners in 1962 with scholarships totaling $3750, to their current level of fifty-nine national scholarships totaling $143,000.

Prior to this invitation to be a judge, I was unaware of this great work that this organization was doing. As I pulled onto the parking lot, I noticed some of the medals that were represented on the license plates of the veterans. It made me proud to be an American. These veterans were now inside totally enjoying the football game, but I am sure there was a time when their lives were on the line for our country and football was the furthest thing from their minds. A little sidebar here—this may not be politically correct, as it seems the words "God Bless" are slowly being regulated out of use but I want to say loud and clear—"God bless" our current armed service personnel and our veterans.

As I listened to the rules on how to judge these young Americans I was curious about what we were would hear from these young people. Well, it didn't take too much listening to conclude they were all terrific. I personally was impressed with their knowledge of current events and, in addition, their creativity of expression. There was great reverence given to veterans, which was to be expected, but to listen to the originality of comments was rewarding. They were all winners but there will be one audio/essay tape representing the state of Missouri that will be sent to Washington to compete in the National finals this coming year.

When the judging was done and I was driving home, I felt really great to have enjoyed the VFW surroundings and the brief conversations I had with Lyle Bonney, a 81-year- young veteran of World War II. This, along with hearing the speeches of these fifteen competing young people, was truly inspiring for this senior and gives hope for the future of our country. It eases my mind that there are young people out there who desire to continue many of our traditions and respect the values of those who have gone before them.

1950-1959
"A Prosperous Time"

Though there were very serious things going on in the world at large, like the Cold War with the Soviet Union and the acceleration of the arms race, for many people in the US, the international tension was balanced by the affordability of creature comforts and a lively economy. Particularly after 1955, we enjoyed high wages, large gas-guzzling cars, and home comforts and time-saving devices like vacuum cleaners and washing machines. This was the decade of prosperity and consumerism, with the advent of credit cards, Madison Avenue ads and Rock'n roll music, America's love affair with the automobile. Just think—gasoline was less than 10 cents a gallon! The two-car family came into existence.

Our modern-day shopping mall had its beginnings in The Northland Center near Detroit, Michigan in 1954. It was the first of its kind to be enclosed and air-conditioned, with 200-300 shops, childcare facilities, restaurants, and plenty of free parking. It was amazingly modern, even by our standards today!

Yes, America was prosperous and leading the world in innovations of all kinds—from development of the polio vaccine to the debut of the *Barbie Doll* and the comic strip called *Peanuts*. Another phenomena that was taking place was the advent of the "teenage generation," recognizing youth between age 13-19 as a people group. This has affected everything from the way products are marketed to how we perceive ourselves in the United States. It hasn't happened all at once, but there has been a radical change in how the young treat their elders. Today, there is a lack of respect shown to older people and a dismissal of the wisdom that has been gained through years of living. The seeds of this mentality were planted in the 1950s, though it would be years before the crop came to full fruition.

SECTION 3

A HERITAGE OF FREEDOM

CHAPTER NINE

Politics

Civility in Politics

I know it used to be true that in polite conversation there were
several topics that were taboo. Two of these were religion and
politics. However, it's probably not true anymore. Besides, how can
we avoid the topics that are so much in the news and bombarding
our households every day of the week? So much for politeness!

One of the areas where politeness is missing is in politics. It is
my opinion that civility and cooperation has disappeared in our
government and politics. We see how politicians try to play "gotcha
politics" by accusing their opponents of misdeeds. Have you noticed
that this is what is in the news today? The more outrageous a statement that is made by a politician, the more attention it is given by the
news media, which only helps stoke the fires of incivility in government. Not only that, there is so much distortion of the truth in the
political arena. Instead of hearing the whole story, with both sides of
an argument presented, we get "sound bites" designed to manipulate
us. In this day of advanced technology in recording equipment, it is
easy to edit out much of the context of what is being said in a particular situation, thus, we are not necessarily seeing "the real thing" as
it happened. These sound bites are then used against an opposing

politician in order to influence voters. This manipulation by the media leaves us asking, "Where is the truth?"

For a moment let's look at an example of incivility in Congress: the congressional nomination process for the appointment of judges to the bench. This process has been totally politicized, in my opinion, as evidenced by the opposing political party's massacre of a candidate's reputation. Instead, there is a need to determine the qualifications of nominees, regardless of party affiliation or other agenda.

The old cycles of politics have disappeared. In years gone by, we had the campaign cycle and then the cycle of governing. Today there is one cycle, which is campaigning all the time. It seems that the elected candidate is always looking to the next election. Now what is the result of this scenario? It seems to me there is hardly any bipartisan cooperation in developing and implementing legislation for the good of the country. It appears that a lot of these politicians are more interested in their political careers than they are in representing their constituents.

I think that there are a lot of good people who would not consider government service because they're unwilling to subject themselves to the personal humiliation that the political process entails.

I feel that the American people are sick and tired of the "gothca politics" that is a result of the lack of civility. I feel that the American electorate would respond well to leaders who have a positive approach and who would keep their promises. Just think how refreshing this would be and, I would venture to say they would become highly successful. This positive approach would become infectious, and then there would be the potential for men and women of integrity to be elected to public office.

We must have healthy partisanship with debate over laws and policies, but it needs to be done with civility. We have a representative democracy, and therefore, our representatives must work together to get things accomplished. Civility is very important, for it is through civility in the public arena that our young people learn how to relate to others, rejecting such tactics as "might makes right" and "whoever shouts the loudest wins."

How is this problem resolved? I think that it starts with leadership. Leaders of all political parties must provide leadership to assure their parties will comply with a high standard of civility. What we need is the "Mr. Smith Goes to Washington" type of individual. You know what? The American people are very perceptive and intelligent. If we could see these changes in the public arena, what a better place this would be to live. And maybe, just maybe, when you ask a youngster what he or she wants to be when he or she grows up, the answer will be, "I want to be President."

* * * * *

Historical Moment from 1960
US gets youngest president ever. By one of the
narrowest margins in American political history,
Democratic Party candidate John F. Kennedy
has been elected president.

* * * * *

Get Out the Vote

One of our great freedoms is the ability to vote for the person we want to be elected for a particular office. We must exercise this freedom whether it is at the local, state or national level. This is your opportunity, so if you don't vote and you don't like the results of the election, don't complain.

Why is the voter turnout so low at election time? There are many reasons for this lack of interest but I want to address one reason, which I have heard many times, and that is, "Elected officials won't listen to us anyway, so why vote?" This attitude may be the surest way to keep the elected official from listening to their constituents. If I am an elected official and I don't hear the loud and consistent voices of my constituents, I am going to do my "thing," which will help me on my own personal career path. Our nation's democracy will be improved when citizens become more involved through voting, communicating with their elected officials and working with their representatives.

Voter turnout has been discussed, with suggestions that we have weekend voting, or perhaps drive-up voting—you know, the "fast food" approach. In other words, let's make it as convenient as possible for the voter. I think what really needs to be changed, however, is voter attitude. As I stated before, as Americans we must get involved in our government's decisions and issues. When we get more involved, this will result in elected officials who will strictly have the interest of the people in mind when decisions are made that affect our lives. One may say this is a pipe dream but I say let's shoot for the moon and, if we fall short, we will at least be better off than we are now. We as grandparents, relatives, fathers, mothers, neighbors and educators should educate the non-voter as to the importance of voting. It does not take that much time to vote but be sure to check the "chads." If you have a neighbor who can't drive to the poll site, offer to drive them. We are blessed to live in a country where we have the freedom to express our viewpoints through voting.

* * * * *

Historical Tidbit from 1971
18 years of age is the new voting age granted to Americans.

* * * * *

We may be turned off by the negative "electioneering," but we should not let that keep us away from the polls. Now it is a given that we have had and always will have tough competition by the politicians to get elected to office. But in recent years I have noted how some will say anything to get elected. They are like trees swaying in the wind.

I would like to share my thoughts on the upcoming presidential election in 2004. Is it that time already? It is hard for us to realize sometimes that there is actually an election coming because there is so much "politicking" going on year round.

I want to offer you a suggestion that will be a lot of fun. When you listen to the persons running for office, pay close attention to what they say. Know their position on issues. Also pay attention to the media person who is interviewing the candidates and take note of the type of questions they ask. Do they consistently ask "hardball" questions or do they ask a mixture of "hardball" and "softball" questions? To me this is very important and will help us to determine if candidates have firm convictions on the issues or if they are like grass blowing in the wind, changing direction depending on the audience of the day.

We must have debate, and throughout the history of elections in our country, these debates have become hot and heavy. This is healthy and that is why we are a country of free people and are the envy of the world. It is the challenge of the voter to determine who is the individual with integrity and supports the voter's views on issues. I will add that today with the decline of social values in our country, we must ask the questions that will help determine the value systems of the candidates. It is hard to ask these types of questions because, as a rule, individual citizens do not get that opportunity. It is my opinion that the media interviewers do not touch that "turf" so that we can hear politicians' answers. So be very attentive and try and determine what kind of value system the politicians really have.

Elections are so important. The elected officials are the ones who create the laws of the country that control our daily lives, so we had better pay attention and not get the attitude of "my vote doesn't count." Well! Do we remember what happened in Florida in the 2000 presidential election? Voting is not a task that we leave for the "other person." You may think you're too busy to vote or that your vote doesn't really matter, but you need to be responsible. Elections can be decided by a small percentage of voters. The percentage of people who vote is amazingly small for a free society. I guess we are all spoiled with having these freedoms and take them for granted. Don't be lulled into complacency. In addition to these elections, keep your eye on proposed legislation and keep track of how your current representatives vote. Some have a tremendous absentee record during the campaign season—which is illogical, for we elected them to represent our views and act accordingly, not to continually be running for office.

Don't be discouraged by all the negative campaigning or fooled into thinking that your vote doesn't count. Instead, use your brain and do your own research as to which candidate is the best person to represent you in government. Then, give this person your whole-hearted support, trusting him/her to be a person of integrity and one who represents your views, regardless of party affiliation.

* * * * *

Historical Moment from 1931
The "Star-Spangled Banner" has become
the official national anthem.
The tune was based on an old English drinking song,
and the words were written in 1814 by Francis Scott Key.

* * * * *

Though in the past we did have controversy regarding our elected officials and their policy issues, for the most part, we had no reason to be overly concerned about moral issues. But back in "good old days," politicians generally were people with integrity and high moral standards. Now I know one could mention the rumors about Jefferson, Roosevelt, Kennedy and so forth. However, their alleged moral misdeeds were not made public, so the populace was not subjected to the details. Had we known about these alleged misdeeds at the time, the history of those days gone past might be written a little differently. So you must weigh the actions against the standards of those relative times. We don't live in a perfect world and I am not naïve enough to think that all politicians are everything they appear to be. Fortunately, we do have some politicians who are people with high moral standards, integrity and commitment, making sure our country continues to enjoy the freedoms that our Constitution declares are the rights of the citizens of the United States.

The bar for moral standards in our society has been lowered to the point now where defenders of these standards say that married politicians who lie about their adulterous behavior is not our business. How can this be true? The character of a person running for any public office must be of the highest caliber. I assume that these people lie about their immoral activity in order to get elected. What if one of these capers involved a person who was trying to find out our government secrets? This is not a conspiracy theory but it has happened throughout history, so why can it not happen again? If they lie about adulterous affairs, they will lie about anything to save their "royal bottoms." It truly amazes me to listen to so-called political experts making excuses for these people who have not only brought shame on themselves but also embarrassment to their families and the nation under their leadership. We should be the role model for other countries, not only for our economic accomplishment and our freedoms, but also as the standard bearer for morality and integrity. If the moral standards decay, everything else will follow. Improper actions by our elected representatives are totally unacceptable. Things like lying should not even be up for discussion. Just recently a proposal was being submitted for consideration for the members of Congress stating that it would be unethical for a congressperson to have an affair with an intern. Think about that. To me that is a no-brainer. Do we have to have guidelines or laws to forbid these types of actions? I thought that was part of the criteria of being elected officials, as they are the standard bearers of morality and integrity for their constituents. Remember, these are the people who are involved with the nation's business. If you can't trust them, whom can you trust? Some political analysts stated that if we eliminated these people from their elected offices, we would be eliminating a lot of the members of Congress. So? Clean house and replace them with people who can focus on the affairs of the country rather than extra-marital affairs. How do we do this? Let the candidates know what you are expecting from them, not only on the issues, but also what you expect from them when it comes to morality and being persons of integrity. Then go vote based on issues and social standards. Hold them accountable for their actions, whether it be lying, stealing, mishandling money, or not being responsible as they decide on legislation.

Finally, we must pay attention to the election of the right people who are responsible for the laws that affect our daily and future lives. We research and deliberate on the expenditure of our personal capital when we buy major ticket items like a home or car. So how about taking the same time and thought when you get ready to make a decision on who you will have representing you at all levels of government, from the lowest elected office to the highest. They are all of relative importance. Remember, you have a vested interest in legislation that deals with you and your family, such as taxes, Social Security, Medicare, environment, etc. Let us consider it a blessing to have a voice in the future of our beloved USA.

* * * * *

Historical Moment from 1951
The 22nd Amendment limits US presidents to two terms in power.

* * * * *

Forces from Without – Are They Winning?

We live in a day and time in which we must place our trust in our elected officials more and more, hence the concern about their integrity. We recognize as never before that our enemies outside our country want to destroy us, and they are doing it on our soil. The horrific events of September 11, 2001 have awakened us to this threat. We are more aware than ever that terrorism is an ever-present reality in this day and age. This is frightening. We wonder if it is safe to take that cruise we planned when we hear reports that cruise ships are potential targets. We have second thoughts about flying to a vacation spot. Perhaps we would like to take the Amtrak to visit Chicago for a weekend of shopping, staying at a beautiful hotel, enjoying a wonderful breakfast, and then touring to see the sights. Or we may want to take a jet to New York to see a Broadway play (to me there is no other entertainment like a Broadway musical). We are trying to live normal lives, making plans for doing things that we enjoy, but in the back of our minds there is the threat that some terrorist group may attack in a public place.

Centers of entertainment have been discussed as potential targets. Please note—I said *potential*. Well, it is my viewpoint that this type of threat should not stop those seniors who travel to seek their entertainment. It will not stop me. Terrorists want to put fear in our hearts to stop us from living normal lives. If we don't continue to live freely because of fearfulness, they have won without ever doing a physical act. Again, terrorism is all about getting into our heads with fear. I say, no way is this going to happen to me!

After all, we face terror everyday when we get on one of the interstate highways and face that group of drivers that I term as "kamikaze pilots." They are not at 30,000 feet in the air but at "ground zero." There are many more daily threats to our lives in the society in which we live today. Why should we stop living a full life because of some *potential* terrorist threats?

How do we overcome crippling fear? Fear is overcome by faith. How many times in your life have you overcome fear by having faith in the Supreme Being. We must not allow our lives to be filled with sleepless nights and tormented days, for we know by experience that faith can calm our fears.

Our senior days are so very precious to us, and every morning when we wake up, we must say to ourselves that we are very happy and blessed. We should be thankful for each day and the privilege to participate in life. Remember, the war on terror is not like World War II when we could identify the enemy and we knew where they were. Today, our enemies are not located in one place and they have many faces and are hard to identify. This being the case, I believe it will take years and years to defeat these enemies. So don't wait for the war on terror to be over before you allow yourself to experience joy and freedom from fear, because if you do, you are going to miss these wonderful and fun-filled days of our golden years.

It may seem frivolous of us to think of fun-filled days in the midst of war and terror, but I think it is one way that we can maintain our sanity. There is nothing pleasant about any war. General William T. Sherman said, "War is hell!"[65] and that quote remains famous because, though it is a simple phrase, it really does say it all.

War is still with us and that war is called the "War on Terrorism," The enemies are without a face and country but there are countries that provide havens for training terrorists and even offer financial support. We know that these outsiders are infiltrating Iraq at an alarming rate, attacking our soldiers. It is even being said that the terrorists are paying families for the use of their sons as suicide bombers.

The United States is aware of these countries and their efforts to undermine the American role in securing freedom for the masses in the Middle East. At the same time, we are acting in self-defense and want to protect our own country from these terrorist regimes.

From news reports we learn about the various tactics our country is pursuing to eliminate the heads of this terrible monster know as terrorism. It is my opinion that we must be patient and support our country in this effort. Remember, these terrorists are hidden and must be rooted out of their dens of evil. It is not like in the past where as a rule, there were battle lines drawn. Yes we had door-to-door combat and guerrilla warfare in the jungles, but we were fighting an enemy force rather than terrorists who are nothing but gangsters hiding among the civilian population. Terrorists are not soldiers but gangsters guilty of multiple murders. They are gangsters and to give them a designation as soldiers gives them too much stature. Some might even call them warriors but to me that is even too much stature.

Prior to 9/11, we were attacked by these gangsters many times, as in the case of the USS Cole bombing and the 1993 World Trade Center attack. But when 9/11 hit our country, it seemed for many of us like the Japanese attack on Pearl Harbor all over again.

In looking back throughout history, it is my opinion that most wars were fought over freedom. This current war is about maintaining our safety and freedoms. This war is different from many other wars, in that we will not wake up every morning and read in the headlines that we just won another major combat battle. This time it will take patience and belief in our leadership that in time we will prevail, and we still are the greatest nation in the world.

We seniors remember when our nation was attacked at Pearl Harbor. We had no armed force to speak of, but we mobilized. Even at first when we did not have tanks, we used trucks and put signs on the side of them saying, "Tank." Yes, as we all know we "improvised and won the battle for freedom" not only for our country but also the world. So, you gangsters, beware, because you are messing with the wrong country!

We are so blessed to have these freedoms and we must fight in our own way to keep these freedoms alive and well. Millions have died so that we may have freedom. I surely don't want us not to be able to have free speech like the people of Iraq, who were just liberated by American armed services and coalition partners. We continue to fight the gangsters who are killing our soldiers in order to return to power. There are stories of homes being wire-tapped to see if anyone was talking against the dictator, Saddam Hussein. We are now hearing stories of children being released from prison who had been put there because they would not do the bidding of Saddam. To me this regime sounds very similar to our enemies in World War II.

Remember Hitler's enforcers called the Gestapo? Remember Herr Goebels, the propaganda minister? Iraq had "Baghdad Bob." I really don't know if we could take him seriously, as he kept stating that Iraq was winning the war. However, if you were observant, you would have seen an American tank as the cameraman moved slightly to the left. I think it is obvious that the Americans are winning the war.

It appears to me that the gangsters hate our freedoms, which is the most valuable asset that we have. Some of these assets are our individual freedoms to live as we choose, to come and go as we please, to worship as we wish and many more freedoms. The air we breathe is freedom.

It is my view that we must not crawl in a cave and hide. So we must—especially our retirees who have worked their whole lives so that they could enjoy the "twilight of their years"—keep those retiree plans. Take those cruises, plane trips and those "snow bird" vacations in the winter. No way will we let these criminals take our happiness away that we earned by working and saving for these golden years.

The War in Iraq and the continuing War on gangsters is painful, bloody and terrible, but as long as we the citizens of this wonderful nation want freedom, it will be a way of life to fight for those freedoms.

Forces from Within – Bringing Back Character

Character: "A quality or trait that distinguish an individual or group"

Quality: "An essential and distinguishing attribute of something or someone."

Does character really matter in our elected officials? These are our elected representatives who create and vote on laws that govern our everyday living. We are a free society and as such must have the very best to carry out their responsibilities.

We have recently had a deluge of scandals involving our politicians. The scandals have reached the highest office in the land and to our congressional representatives. Some who have been caught have resigned their positions and others have been evasive. One in particular—the former President of the United States William Jefferson Clinton (when accused of adulterous behavior)—was less then forthcoming. He will probably go down in history as arguing the definition of the word "is" as it relates to the definition of sex. Of course he will also go down in history as being impeached—all because he didn't exhibit a high standard of morality and character. Now the backers of the President were ever present on television and quoted in major newspapers, maintaining that what he did in his private life had no relevancy to performing his duties as the President of the United States of America, the most powerful nation in the world. The denial by the President, his wife (stating on television that it was a "right wing conspiracy") and supporters continued until the evidence clearly showed his guilt. Although he publicly apologized to the American people, there was no sign of sincere repentance, but rather he continued to give excuses for his behavior, still maintaining that what he did in his private life had no bearing on his job performance.

Along with the debacle of Clinton's impeachment, we saw the resignation of Speaker of the House Newt Gingrich from Congress as it was found out he was having an affair. Rather than face total embarrassment, he elected to resign. Bob Livingston, who was the potential candidate to follow Newt Gingrich as the Speaker of the House, also was found guilty of having an affair and immediately resigned to avoid certain embarrassment.

Remember Gary Condit (California Congressman) who was accused of being a sexual predator? Not only that, there was a cloud over his head in his possible involvement in the disappearance of Chandra Levy, an intern in Washington DC. This news disappeared due to the September 11, 2001 World Trade Center (WTC) atrocities. But due to the WTC and the lack of media attention, he decided to run for office again. Remember, he was a member of the newly formed Home Defense Committee. Fortunately, the voting public pronounced their judgment on his behavior and lack of character by voting him out of office by a huge margin.

The proponents of this sexual permissiveness as it relates to the private lives of public officials state that this has been going on since the days of Washington. If we are going to point to the past for justification of current behavior, why not look at those who did uphold high standards? Here are some quotes from prominent Americans of the past:

> Virtue and vice will not grow together in a great degree, but they will grow where they are planted, and when one has taken root, it is not easily supplanted by the other. The great art of correcting mankind consists in prepossessing the mind with good principles. – Noah Webster [6]

> We in the business world don't want young people coming into our employment and into our communities who are brilliant, but dishonest; who have great intellectual knowledge, but don't really care about others; who have highly creative minds, but are irresponsible. All of us in business and the entire adult community need to do our part in helping build young people of high character. There isn't a more critical issue in education today. – Sanford N. McDonnell, Chairman Emeritus of the former McDonnell Douglas Corporation.

My argument is that character does count. In the pre-Clinton era, the media did not point out scandals such as John Kennedy's alleged womanizing and his most famous alleged affair with Hollywood starlet Marilyn Monroe. In fact, the media was very protective of our leadership in the past. For example, they avoided taking pictures, if at all possible, of President Franklin Roosevelt in his wheelchair, as he was crippled by polio.

Why did the media start revealing these scandals? It is my contention that, due to the scandals of Clinton prior to his election and passionate denials by him and his wife, there arose a need for investigative reporting. Of course, the political opposition use scandalous behavior of their opponents as a means to get attention in the media—not to mention the attempt by the media to rise in the ratings.

I make the argument that character does count as one of the job requirements to be an elected official who represents "We the People" of these United States. We are a free society and need the very best to make the laws and uphold our constitution in order for us to maintain our freedoms.

Who is to say that if the media had exposed those alleged scandals while those "tainted politicians" were in office what our history would be today.

Now that our society has been eroded with this apparent acceptance of a politician's character that lying and sexual permissiveness is okay, where are we headed? Character does count, and this is not just from a religious point of view. Exhibiting character is a requirement for every one of us if we are going to be able to trust and love others and work together as the human race. This is the only way we can continue to exist in an open, loving and free society.

I believe that if a person would cheat and lie to his family, he will lie to the citizens of the United Sates to protect his job and achieve his personal goals. People like this would, in my opinion, sacrifice the good of the country in order to save their reputations and their economic welfare. In addition, it is my opinion that their egos are so great they would lie and distort to save their so-called legacy. If we kicked out of office those who continue their misdeeds, we might get people who would actually work together. This would allow nonpartisan debate. Maybe our politicians would have as a motto "Country First"—how about that? Now we should always have debate, but let's have it without political hidden agendas.

What can we do as citizens? We should ask the questions relative to character such as:

- What is your opinion relative to adultery?
- What is your definition of character as it relates to holding a political office?
- What action would you take against any peer who you found lying, cheating or having an adulteress affair?
- Name your political role models and why.
- Finally, does character count even as it relates to your private life?

In summary, we must have people in office who can devote their time to affairs of our country and not to covering up scandals in their private lives. Again, if you have the ability to lie and commit actions that you hide from the world, you are not qualified to represent the citizens of the United States.

How Taxing!

I have given the following topic much thought and have had many discussions with friends and relatives on the issue of cigarettes' and related things' being taxed. As a result I want to provide you with some of my views regarding this topic for you to consider and you can derive your own conclusions. Cigarette prices have gone through the roof in past years. By the way, I don't smoke any form of tobacco. I understand that the increase in the price of cigarettes is due primarily to two things. First are the high state taxes and the multibillion-dollar tobacco settlement against the major tobacco corporations. I noticed on one sign of a local discount tobacco store that a carton cost twenty-five dollars plus. I understand that in California, which is up to their chins in state budgetary problems (along with a majority of our states) that cigarettes are costing more than thirty-eight dollars a carton.

Public places are now banning the smoking of cigarettes. I heard of a case where one neighbor was suing his next door neighbor because the smoke from his house was drifting over to his house—thus endangering his household with second-hand smoke. Yes I heard this story. Is it true? I don't know but as for as I am concerned, in this era of suing one another for the most minor of things from burning your lap with a hot cup of coffee to whatever— it is believable!

Now if smoking cigarettes causes cancer, then why is it legal? We know that taking dope will deprive you of your mental capabilities and eventually will kill you. It is considered addictive and dangerous to your health and thus we have laws that say possession and taking of narcotics is illegal. The government spends billions of dollars every year to shut down drug trafficking and the rehabilitation of the drug addict. An addict is "a person with a habit so strong that they cannot easily give it up," according to Webster's Dictionary. We even have a "drug czar" to manage this problem and we have an agency, the DEA, that is dedicated to running down these criminals in order to protect our citizens from having access to narcotics, which is against the law.

Narcotics can prevent you from having your complete senses while driving a car or handling equipment, and if not handled properly, can endanger the health or even life of someone. Now on the other hand, smoking a cigarette does not carry that danger unless you drop it on your lap while driving and you run into someone or smoke gets in your eyes, causing you to take your eye off the road at a critical moment.

The point I want to make is—if smoking can kill you, why not ban smoking just like illegal drugs and send people to jail? Think about that! Do you think there is hidden economic reason for some that smoking is not banned? I noticed that during the budget battles, it is not uncommon to hear someone recommend they increase the taxes on cigarettes to help with their monetary problems. Now these taxes are passed onto the consumer, as the tobacco industries are not going to eat these costs. I guess, in a way, we are increasing taxes on the tobacco smoker. I have always said we have freedom of choice and, if you want to smoke, be my guest. Tobacco kills, but I guess killing is okay as long as it doesn't interfere with free enterprise and the profit of the powerful.

We live in a land where consumerism looms large and free

enterprise is the basis of our economy. I don't think any of us wants to give up the freedoms that come with this kind of society, but I do believe that we need to voice our concerns, getting the attention of the politicians who are representing us. We also need to use common sense in our own chosen lifestyles. We need to refocus in this country. For too long we have capitulated to the demands of individuals (or small minority groups) and have forgotten to do what is best for the whole of society. We need to choose the greater good, even if it means personal sacrifice of our instant gratification mentality. For two hundred years of our nation's history there was a pride and patriotism in our way of life, but both national pride and patriotism seem to be fading today. In our rush to be "pluralistic," we have not only tolerated terrorists living in our land who are plotting our destruction, we have allowed those who have no integrity or sense of morality to destroy us from within. It is time to reverse the tide. It will take all of us, from the heroic WWII generation to the youth of the current generation—paying attention, contributing our minds and talents, upholding tried and true standards, and blazing the trail into the future.

* * * * *

Politically Correct Holiday Greetings

Please accept with no obligation, expressed or implied, my best wishes for an environmentally conscious, socially responsible, low stress, non-addictive, gender-neutral celebration of the winter-solstice holiday, practiced within the most enjoyable traditions of the religious persuasion or secular practices of your choice—with respect, of course, for the religious/secular persuasions and/or traditions of others, or for their choice not to practice religious or secular traditions at all.

And a fiscally successful, personally fulfilling, and medically uncomplicated recognition of the onset of the generally accepted calendar year, but not without due respect for the calendars-of-choice of other cultures whose contributions to society have helped make America great—not to imply that America is necessarily greater than any other country or is the only AMERICA in the western hemisphere—and without regard to the race, creed, color, age, physical ability, religious faith, or choice of computer platform of the recipient.

(Source Unknown)

* * * * *

CHAPTER TEN

Entertainment

Entertainment is a big part of our lives in American culture. It comes in many forms and is defined by the individual's interpretation of what entertainment is for him. In this section we will address the more common forms of entertainment such as movies, sports, reading, television, concerts, and the Internet.

* * * * *

Historical Tidbit from 1966
Hollywood launched the TV series *Star Trek* that set out "to boldly go" where no man has gone before.

* * * * *

In the '30s, '40s, '50s, and '60s, entertainment, from my point of view, was very simple, non-threatening and for the whole family to enjoy as a unit. All movies were "G" rated, though we did not feel we needed a rating system. There were actually even those in the movie industry who censured what was allowed on the "big screen." Today that would not be politically correct and somebody would call "foul" and probably take the producers to court.

In the sports arena we had a lot of heroes. Although there were isolated scandals and corruption, these were the exceptions rather than the common occurrences that we see today. It seems that we as a society have become shock proof. In my day, we had a lot of role models representing all sports that we could all look up to. Remember the baseball cards? For the most part, these were people (at least as far as we knew) of integrity.

Magazines were "G" rated and were displayed on the top of the counter for all to see. It's amazing today to look at some of the covers of prestigious magazines advertising articles that in my opinion are "R" rated. If the titles are offensive, I wonder what the content would be!

There are exceptions to this trend, however, and if you really want to find wholesome entertainment, you can. For example, my wife and I recently attended a high school play entitled the "Sound of Music," which was sheer delight. The work that was put into this production by the students and adults was quite evident. I had no relatives participating in this event, but having had all of my children participate in school activities and now my grandchildren, I wanted to see what was "happening." My wife and I had a wonderful Sunday afternoon with the best of entertainment. This is good and we compliment the people responsible for these events. We need more of these similar types of events with community and family participation. By the way, the cast got a standing ovation. It gave me the proverbial "goose bumps."

Remember when there was no television or the Internet? If you do, you're certainly showing your age here. The purity of the radio waves brought us the news (with newscasters like Walter Winchell, Jimmy Fiddler and H. V. Kaltenborn). We were entertained by the episodes of the "Green Hornet," The "Phantom" and "Gang Busters."

* * * * *

Historical Tidbit from 1938
On Halloween, *War of the Worlds*, a highly realistic play
about a Martian invasion of New Jersey, was broadcast.
In the US, listeners responded to the play as
if it were a live news report, causing a panic.

* * * * *

Now what do we have today? Let's take sports. It has been invaded with abuse of drugs and steroids, resulting in suspensions, fines and other image destroying action. This is the day of the big paychecks and bonuses based on performance (I thought that's what they got paid for in the first place!). I want to see the athlete who plays for the sport of the game, not for how much money he makes. Sports fans know who these real athletes are—we can spot them and, in my opinion, they are rare today. In the "good old days," these kinds of players were the norm and I am proud to have been a part of that era.

* * * * *

Historical Tidbit from 1972
First home video recorder marketed.
This machine can record and play
back TV movies using a special tape cassette
that records TV signals.

* * * * *

Movies are so bad today that we have developed categories such as "G" for family viewing up to the category of "R," which is restricted for viewing by the adult members of the family. In my opinion, no member of the family should view the movies rated "R." Why? The nudity, explicit sex, language and violence, for which these movies are rated, are not conducive to a wholesome society. Many will argue the first amendment, "freedom of expression," "form of art" and so forth. But again—in my opinion—if we can't let our children view something because it is not good for them in their formative ages, why do we think it's good for us? We want them to grow up to be ladies and gentlemen, but if the adults around them do not have good discernment concerning entertainment, this is unlikely to happen.

Television and the Internet are a great source of timely local, national and international news, knowledge and entertainment. But again we have the "creeping" sex, language and violence coming into our homes to the point where we have to "lock out" programs in order for children to view television. If we have to lock out viewing material—is it good for anyone?

In the perspective of "then" and "now," what can we do (even in a small way) to have a reality check when it comes to wholesome entertainment? We must be the role models and the educators. As a role model you will earn the credibility to educate those over whom you have influence. I believe in free speech and all of our freedoms. However, I feel that we must monitor the expression of those freedoms by encouraging the best and disregarding the worst.

In the early days of television, we enjoyed programs like "Texaco Theater with Uncle Miltie," "Red Skelton Show," "Twilight Zone," and "The Lucy Show." "The Ed Sullivan Show" was wonderful, as it introduced us to new talent as well as already noted celebrities. How about Julius La Rosa who played the accordion on the "Arthur Godfrey Show?" There was a variety of entertainment that could be viewed by the whole family. No ratings or blocking devices were needed.

Today anything goes. I mean anything! We have reality shows that try to match up couples, have "Big Brother" watching every move of the contestants, artificially created situations in which people "survive," and dramas that seem to outdo each other in how gory they can be. I cannot tell you what the real theme is in most of these shows, as I don't watch them once I see where they are going. There are some programs where the violence is unbelievable. To me, for the networks to air this type of programming is totally irresponsible and explains why people are becoming so desensitized—especially the younger generation.

We also have shows that prey on the unfortunate (i.e. the "Jerry Springer Show"), and these types of shows have high ratings. This, to me, says that society accepts this type of programming and, in fact, wants more. Now it has been my experience in talking to seniors over the past few years that this is not acceptable for my generation that grew up in the 30s, 40s and 50s. This type of programming is not only an outrage but highly offensive and it is absent of values that we hold dear—morality, integrity and character.

Perhaps our concerns are being taken seriously by some because, when it comes to national elections, we see some of the politicians coming out against the movie and television industry, urging them to clean up their movies and programming. However, you may notice that the outcry is only temporary and after the elections, business goes on as usual. Occasionally we do get a statistical update. Wow, that is really great! Give me a break and quit trying to pacify us with your effort of statistical analysis.

Having said all that, I believe that the entertainment and print media should do an about-face and start contributing to this society in a positive way. Let's get rid of the immoral programming and go back to the time of "G" rated programming, whether it be on television, in movies or in reading material. This entertainment could be the catalyst in delivering wholesome entertainment in all venues. This entertainment could be seen by the whole family, providing opportunities for mixed age groups to interrelate and older generations to have an influence on the young.

Where are we headed? Today we have obscenity displayed on cars and trucks and car radios blasting obscene music, not to mention "angst" expressed on T-shirts, etc. Am I a cranky old senior? I don't think so. What can we seniors do about this dismal trend we see in our country? Express your dismay at every opportunity you get. And remember, when it comes to election time, ask our politicians not only how they stand on these issues but what are they going to do about it. After they are elected, follow up on their legislative actions, and let that be your guide in voting in the next election. Let's hold our elected officials accountable for their voting records. We need people in office who will not only represent those of us who have strong moral values, but will also be a positive force for getting our country back on track.

Good News/Bad News

Remember back in the '30s and '40s when we got our news by the radio and the newspaper? I remember as a child growing up in the rural area of Missouri when we got the news primarily by radio. If my memory serves me right, we got a newspaper once a week.

The good old Zenith radio gave us the news by our favorite commentators.

The whole family would gather around the radio to listen. Sometimes the news was earth-shaking, like we got on Sunday December 7, 1941, a "day of infamy" when the Japanese's attacked Pearl Harbor. In our family, we got a phone call to turn on the radio. I remember everyone gathering around the radio in disbelief that anyone would attack the United States. I also remember the weeks that followed when the young men went to the draft boards that had been set up to sign up as volunteers to fight the enemy.

Not only did we hear the news, but we also listened to the radio for our entertainment. I remember listening to the ball games with such stars as Enos Slaughter and Pepper Martin. In addition, we had a colorful radio announcer by the name of Dizzy Dean who would say "he slud into third base," which brought some degree of protest from English teachers. Boy! Times surely have changed from that outrage over something so minor to today's acceptance of any form of speech as long as it is politically correct.

Now compare that period of time to what we have today to get our national and international news. Not only do we have the radio and newspapers but now television and the Internet. To me, the fastest way to get the global news is the Internet. A case in point there is a story that happened years ago. There was a scandal involving the highest office in the land and it was first reported on the Internet. It took some time before it was news in the mainstream news media. Today I can go on the Internet and get the news, and when I go to listen to the news in the evening, it is already old news. Also, I cannot get the full story, as broadcasters are constrained by air time. Actually, we rarely get the full story because most broadcast news is quite biased, usually from a liberal slant.

In the good old days, life was much slower and simpler. We did not quickly get news of events happening across the globe and I think overall there was just more decency in our society. Today we have a society with so many more ills, resulting in so many news stories related to entertainment figures involved in sex scandals, corporate corruption, political scandals, wars throughout the world, terrorism, and the list goes on and on.

It is my opinion that we seniors must keep informed on what is happening in the world. We have interests in such topics as Medicare, Social Security and issues relating to social values. We must continue to be involved in our elections, as we are voting for people who will not only have an impact on our lives but our children's lives. For instance, the political party that is in power has the opportunity to appoint Supreme Court judges, who have these positions for life and make far-reaching decisions affecting every facet of our lives. Just think of all the millions of babies that have been aborted since 1973 when judges on the Supreme Court ruled abortion to be legal. So, seniors, stay up with the news and speak out when you find biased reporting, too much violence portrayed, and endless debate over some public figure's scandal.

Going to the Movies

Do you remember when all movies were appropriate for the whole family? There was a time when you got two movies, World News and some cartoons for thirty-five cents. Plus, you could get a box of popcorn and some Milk Duds or Switzer Licorice for less than the price to get into the movies. You would eat the popcorn during the first movie and the candy during the second flick.

Also we would take all of our children to the show and they would sit there like little gentlemen and women. Grandma, as a rule, would go with us. There were times an aunt who was widowed would also go along. It was a family affair. We had neighborhood theaters to which you could walk, and this was a pleasure, as we could "window shop" along the way. For example, passing the drugstore, we could see the bargains displayed in the window. Sometimes, instead of getting the popcorn and candy at the show, on the way home, we would stop in at the drugstore, sit down at a metal table or at the counter, and have the "soda jerk" make us a root beer float, or maybe a banana split or a chocolate malt. Also, they would serve two little cookies to enjoy with the drink. We always planned a certain day of the week, which for us was Friday, as children did not have to go to school the next day. As I write this, I can't help but think about how simple and pure these days were in raising a family in the '40s and '50s. As I look back on those days of family life and raising our children, I remember it as being uncomplicated and totally enjoyable. It was clean, safe, and above all, it was totally family-centered.

Back then, going to the movies had another side benefit. The Movie House would have give-away items such as dinnerware. Over a period of weeks you could get a whole set of dishes by just going to the movies. Now for the everyday person this was a blessing and it was enjoyable to see and listen to the ladies discuss how their dish collections were progressing.

Now to the movies we saw. I would like to start off with some cowboy movie stars of the past just to tickle your memory bank. How about this list—Tom Mix, Buck Jones, Johnny Mack Brown, Hopalong Cassidy, Red Ryder, Gene Autry, Roy Rogers and then latter Marshall Matt Dillon and there were more. It's my belief that these were role models on the movie screen for us who were growing up in the '30s and '40s and these heroes helped build our generation's societal values base. These values of our heroes are worthy of emulating, so don't worry if somebody refers to our current president as a "cowboy." There was a great piece on the Internet that was forwarded to me, referring to the common attributes these cowboys shared. This is the list, plus some other commentary about some of our contemporary heroes:

1. They were never looking for trouble.

2. But when trouble came, they faced it with courage.

3. They were always on the side of right.

4. They defended good people against bad people.

5. They had high morals.

6. They had good manners.

7. They were honest.

8. They spoke their minds and they spoke the truth, regardless of what people thought or "political correctness," which no one had ever heard of back then.

9. They were a beacon of integrity in the wild, wild West.

10. They were respected. When they walked into a saloon (where they usually drank only sarsaparilla), the place became quiet, and the bad guys kept their distance.

11. If in a gunfight, they could outdraw anyone. If in a fist fight, they could beat up anyone.

12. They always won. They always got their man. In victory, they rode off into the sunset.

Those were the days when there was such a thing as right and wrong—something blurred in our modern world, and denied by many.

Now, as a senior citizen, I still like cowboys—they represent something good—something pure that America has been missing.

Ronald Reagan was a cowboy.

I like Ronald Reagan, who was brave, positive, and who gave us hope. He wore a white hat. To the consternation of his liberal critics, he had the courage to call a spade a spade and call the former Soviet Union what it was—the evil empire. Liberals hated Ronald Reagan.

They also hate President Bush because he distinguishes between good and evil.

He calls a spade a spade, and after 9-11 called evil "evil," without mincing any words, to the shock of the liberal establishment. That's what cowboys do, you know.

He also told the French to "put their cards on the table" (old West talk), which they did, exposing their cowardice and greed.

The radical Muslims are wrong.

In the old West, might did not make right.

Right made might.

Cowboys in white hats were always on the side of right, and that was their might.

I am glad my President is a cowboy.

He got his man! [Saddam Hussein]

Cowboys do, you know.

(Source Unknown)

****

Entertaining Musicals

How about the movie musicals? They are practically non-existent today. I'm sure we all remember the dancing of Cyd Charisse in her role in "Singing in the Rain," also starring Debbie Reynolds, Donald O'Connor and the fabulous Gene Kelly. The music from this movie has become a classic. In fact, there is a major grocery store today that plays the tune "Singing in the Rain" while spraying some of their vegetables. I feel like grabbing an umbrella and running down the isle and singing "just singing in the rain" myself. I imagine the younger generation does not know the significance of that song that represents an era of musicals long gone by. I consider that a shame. The scenery and extras that made the musicals so enormous and exciting made me glad to have been in the audience back in those days.

When it comes to the classics, we have to remember the movie

"Citizen Kane" that was a groundbreaking cinematic masterpiece and remains as fresh and exciting as its initial release in 1941. So great was the genius of Orson Wells, not only as the star and director, but his behind-the-scenes technical creativity. Then there was the supporting cast of some of the greats such as Joseph Cotten, Agnes Moorehead, and Everett Sloan.

There is so much more to write about the movies of our era but space does not permit me to continue. But I hope you are remembering some of the movies and actors that were your favorites as you grew up in the '30s and '40s. I know I feel blessed to have experienced clean and wholesome movie entertainment that did not require ratings.

A Funny Thing Happened on the Way to the....

The stand-up comedian for family entertainment has disappeared. One of the last of these great comedians recently celebrated his 100th birthday and then died this past year. His name was Bob "thanks for the memories" Hope.

Just think how we use to watch such comedians as Red Skelton, Uncle Miltie, Sid Ceasar, Henny Youngman, Jack Benny, Fibber McGee and Molly, Fred Allen and there are so many more. They knew how to make you laugh. But the one thing they had in common was that their jokes and routines were clean and they were for family viewing.

Most of the shows were filmed live and sometimes the bloopers and reactions from the comedian's partner on stage drew 'belly laughs" that would bring tears to your eyes. I loved to watch Red Skeleton interact with his guests (the show was broadcast live). I thought he was so natural and he made his guests just burst out laughing. I really don't think it was staged, but if it was, they fooled a lot of my friends and me. I remember that on a Monday at the water cooler how each one of us would quote a scene from a show that we had seen over the weekend and the laughter started all over again.

Also the comedy shows not only had a funny "headliner," but they were supported with a cast of funny people—like Art Carney on the "Honeymooners," Salley Struthers in "All in the Family," and entertainers like Phyllis Diller and Jerry Colona on the "Bob Hope Show."

A lot of these comedy shows always had their own bands, such as Les Brown's, the band leader of renown with Bob Hope. It was also common to see Harry James, another bandleader on the shows.

Now what do we have today? Well, the stand-up comedians that I have tuned in to have some of the most vulgar language come out of their mouths that I had ever heard in my life. When I hear this, I immediately turn off the program. The sad part is that the audience is laughing about this smut they are hearing. Not only do their routines not leave anything to the imagination, they seem to come up with things that many of us would not even begin to imagine in our worst nightmares.

Now I am an advocate of free speech, for which some of our Armed Service personnel have died, and I want this freedom to continue. I just hope and pray that these so-called comedians will clean up their mouths and acts and represent the advanced society that we are supposed to be. Networks should make the effort to get some culture and class back into entertainment so that it can be clean and wholesome and something the whole family can watch. Comedians can add to our health, as laughter is a healer. It has been said that what comes out of your mouth is who you are.

We are supposed to be an intelligent progressive society, which we are when it comes to technology and the sciences, but based on the performances of so-called stand-up comedians of today, it is my view that we have digressed to the stage of total immorality. Hopefully there are some stand-up comedians out there performing with clean material that the whole family can enjoy but I am unaware of them. If they are out there, I wish for them all the luck in their careers and hopefully we will see the likes of them on prime time television so the whole family can enjoy clean humor just like we did with "Lucy and Ricky" in the '50s and '60s.

Games People Play

Entertainment for children often consists of very simple, unsophisticated things like games. A summertime game that we played was called the "water balloon war," where the ultimate weapons were balloons filled with water. We chose sides and had a water balloon fight, with the objective of conquering the enemy's fort. It was harmless and very refreshing when you were soaked with water during those hot days of summer.

Wintertime was great for other kinds of games like snowball fights. This involved a lot of the kids. There was much preparation for this "War of Wars." We built forts made of blocks of snow. After the snow forts were made we made our respective flags: "skull and crossbones," "stars and stripes" and many other designs. Now came the preparation of the ammunition. There were several rules in making these snowballs. No ice balls and no rocks could be embedded in the weapon of war—the snowball. Another rule was we fought from our respective forts. When a snowball hit a person, he/she was eliminated. The winning team was the one that had the most players left at the end of the game. The end of the game was determined either by loss of daylight, time for chores or just exhaustion from the exercise and the cold. This game was played at school recess, weekends (time permitting), and sometimes after school as the fort structures stayed until they melted.

Our younger readers might think that the children of the '30s and '40s were violent. On the contrary, we were not violent. The above two games consisted of balloons and snowballs. They consisted of our homemade rules. Now once in awhile one would get hit with a snowball in the face, and that did hurt, but I can't remember anyone receiving an injury. The hit just stung like heck due to the coldness.

In the summer, catching fireflies could happily occupy an entire evening. Parents would sit out on the porch and watch the children catching fireflies (sometimes called lighting bugs). We would get a fruit jar and punch holes in the lid and then go on the hunt for the ever-evasive bug. At the end of the evening, the bugs were released to become the challenge of being caught again and everyone enjoyed the light they gave off.

How about spinning in a circle, getting dizzy, and falling down? We did this just for giggles. How about playing marbles? You would draw the circle and try to shoot your opponent's marble out of the ring, resulting in your owning the marble. There were marbles that were considered to be the "shooters" that could make you the keeper of many bags of marbles. Many little thumbs got very sore.

* * * * *

What is the deal with lightning bugs?

I mean, here is this rather ordinary looking flying insect, but wait…it has a glow-in-the-dark rear end! What was God thinking?

I'm sure science has all kinds of explanations about how this fluorescent fanny is useful for mating and other stuff, but why did God choose to make the lightning bug glow?

There may be some crucial purpose for the lightning bug that I don't know about, but I have a feeling it may be quite simple.

I wonder if when God was creating all the animals and everything around us, He came up with the idea of the lightning bug and said, "The kids are gonna love these."

We know that God loves us enough to create all the things we need to survive, but does God love us so much He created some things just to make us smile?

Just seeing lightning bugs takes me back to those warm summer nights of my youth. I'd be running around the back yard with my empty Mason jar, racing toward the flashing lights all around me. I can still feel the joy and hear the laughter echoing through my memories.

Lightning bugs were as much a part of summer as fireworks, fresh tomatoes,

and big ice-cold slabs of juicy watermelon.

God created so much diversity in this world, much more than is needed for mere survival. He made all of this for us, and He wants us to enjoy it. We can get so busy surrounding ourselves with man-made goods that we don't notice

the living tapestry God has laid out all around us.

I guess lightning bugs do have a purpose after all. They are a reminder of a creative God who loves us so much, He'd even paint the rear end of a bug....just to see us smile!

(Author Unknown)
(Sing this to the old Mills Brothers' tune:" Glowworm")

* * * * *

How about step ball—hitting the ball on the front steps to score runs? Each player was allowed three outs. An out was to miss catching the ball as it flew off the step. We played nine innings. It is my understanding one the greatest St. Louis Cardinal shortstops, who is in the hall of fame, played step ball as a youngster. In retrospect, it was a fantastic game for developing hand and eye coordination.

Remember bottle caps? This, as a rule, was played at the neighborhood tavern. A converted broom handle became a bat. The good pitchers could make those bottle caps do magical things. The curve, and the drop were the more prevalent pitches, at least in my neighborhood.

Cork ball was another favorite. We had leagues of cork ball teams. Bats, gloves and balls were made for the cork ball players. These games were played at the neighborhood taverns as well as other playing areas.

How about Indian ball? Two markers designated the inbound playing field. Grounders that were missed were a hit. Grounders caught were considered an out. Fly balls dropped were a hit. Fly balls caught were an out. A ball hit over the outfielder's head was a home run. And the game was played for as many innings as the players wanted. We played with a softball and regular bats. I remember the parks were filled with many Indian ball games being played. What a delightful time! Certain games drew a lot of spectators.

Finally, do you remember the game called "king of the hill?" That was not a game for me, as I was not that big and the "big boys" would send me rolling down the hill. The object of the game was to try to rush "the king" and try to eliminate his reign by sheer numbers. It was a lot of fun.

Today there is not as much participation in outdoor games, except in organized sports with overbearing coaches and parents demanding that their children be champs. Whatever happened to just playing for fun? I do miss those games of yesterday which, when I think back, brought so much joy to the families and communities.

On the Road Again—Traveling for Entertainment

Way back when, in the time of the Great Depression, families did not know what a vacation was. If a vacation can be defined as time off work, then the many who lost their jobs were on vacation! But was it fun and entertaining? No! Their time was taken up in trying to find a job—from selling Fuller Brush products to encyclopedias—or anything to put bread on the table. Then came the war and there was no vacationing because of gas rationing. Remember the cars that had those "A," "B" and "C" stickers on their windshields to show your rating to get gas at the pump? So walking and public transportation were the primary means of getting around. Walking was not for exercise but the way to get to those job opportunities. Additionally, we were at war and no one was in the mood to vacation, with all of our men and women of the military in "harms way." After the war there were educational and employment opportunities, with prosperity that was evidenced by a boom in house building. It was time for the returning veterans to get home to their families. There were those who got married and started their families. Vacations still were not a priority.

For many, building upon the foundation of the family required most of their waking hours. Dads worked at their jobs and moms had the important job of running the home and primary responsibility for the care and feeding of the children (a 24/7 job). More dads not only had regular jobs but part-time jobs in order to support their families. Also, in addition to the two jobs, they went to night school to obtain their advanced education in order to advance in the job market. I don't know the statistics regarding the size of families, but if my memory serves me right, the families were larger in the '30s and late '40s and early '50s. As I remember, we also had 48-hour workweeks. So a vacation was not one of the family's top priorities.

Vacations have dramatically changed since those years. My experience with business has been that we achieve the ability to take three weeks' vacation more rapidly than in the past. Some people, based on their experience and the company's needs, are hired with four weeks' vacation as one of the hiring incentives. Five-week vacations are even commonplace now.

Three-day weekend holidays have been added, making more free time for travel. Some companies even provide personal days that one can use at his own discretion. We have time off for emergencies that does not take away from our vacation time.

We have introduced another term called flextime, which enables a person to create a work schedule that is more suitable for his/her lifestyle. In some cases, this provides the employee with a three-day weekend.

The "virtual office" gives certain employees such as technology specialists the ability to work from their homes rather then going to the office everyday. This to me eliminates travel time to and from work, preparation time for going to the office everyday, and the ability to manage work time and personal time during the workday. It can also reduce restaurant costs by having the ability to eat at home. One can also save money on that expensive coffee that has become a very frequent indulgence for the worker. Companies derive a benefit as well, such as reducing office and parking space and creating a positive attitude towards the job.

What a transition that has taken place. This is great! We have come a long way when it comes to the ability to enjoy life. So, use that time wisely as every moment of your life is so important.

Other Fun Stuff

Let's reminisce and smile as we travel back in time and recollect words that represent a whole bunch of memories. Recently, on a Saturday morning, I was getting a haircut at my favorite barbershop in old town Florissant. The barber and I started discussing some of the things we enjoyed in our youth. Well, the first thing you know, other customers were joining in the discussion. They even mentioned some things with which I was not familiar. It made for an enjoyable haircut time, reflecting on memories with my senior barber and others in the shop.

Remember candy cigarettes? They were made in the form of a cigarette with a red tip representing the lighted end. I remember having this box of candy cigarettes, pretending to smoke, but that didn't last long because the taste of that pure sugar made me eat the whole thing. So much for the "sophisticate image!" These were imported by some of my relatives from the big city for us country folks. But they definitely were a treat and they were rather sticky, as I remember.

There were also wax coke-shaped bottles with colored sugar water inside. Now I really never cared for the sugar water but I enjoyed chewing the wax because it took the place of chewing gum. Now this was a treat, because when I was on my way to town in the summer time, I would pull some loose tar from the black top road and chew it as if it were gum. I guess we lived in an era when the environment was not contaminated.

How about the soda pop machines that dispensed glass bottles? When you were done, you placed the empty bottle into a wooden soda container. I remember one of my favorite bottles of soda was Nehi orange soda. Royal Crown soda was another favorite. Actually, because they were in glass bottles, I think the flavor was better.

* * * * *

Historical Tidbit from 1916
A very unusual bottle appeared in the stores, bars and diners this summer, when the Coca-cola Company started to sell its fizzy drink in a curvy bottle. The bottle is based on the shape of the cola nut, one of the drink's "secret" ingredients. The owners hope that the unusual shape will help them sell more drinks.

* * * * *

When a weapon was found in our possession at school, it was immediately taken away from us forever. I must confess that our weapons of choice were called sling shots and pea shooters. We never brought another favorite called the "cork popgun" to school, because that was only for the little kids.

Eating for Pleasure

Do you remember metal ice cube trays with levers? It was a great invention, as there was no more chipping away at an ice block to get shavings of ice to make your cold drink. It was great to have the uniformed cube. However, if you did not fill the tray correctly, you would get all types of distorted cubes.

The fast food places of our time, such as the Parkmoore in our town, were the places we "hung out" when we were in High School. They had the tableside jukeboxes. Selection of the song to play was a tedious task due to the lack of funds, so we were very deliberate in this task. Our idea of having a good time was to drink a cherry coke, ice cream soda, thick malt or other drink and an order of French fries while listening to the jukebox and conversing with our friends. Sometimes when we had extra money and we could get a cheeseburger.

Then there were the drive-in movies. They had the playground for the children to use prior to the movie's starting. We had the concession stand with anything from sandwiches to popcorn. I know that we brought most of our treats from home because we had a car full of people, and we needed to save the money, but there were occasions that we availed ourselves of the concession stands. Wintertime presented a problem due to the number of people in the car fogging up the windows, but we were inventive and took care of that problem.

Entertainment for Seniors

There are so many other things that entertained us back in the good old days. I am sure some of you could write stories about your own experiences. It is great to remember the old pastimes, and those of us from earlier eras learned to be entertained by simple pleasures. This has prepared us for a time in our lives now when we call ourselves "seniors."

As seniors we have learned to take pleasure in things like just watching the rain fall. These pleasures are truly blessings that are given to us to enjoy, and it saddens me to see modern-day youth rush through life at such a harried pace that they cannot enjoy these things.

The following are some of the pleasures that I recognize. Maybe you share the same ones. We must enjoy the blessings of the simple things in life if we want to experience contentment. I know that after having a hard physical workout, I feel tired and dripping wet, but when I get into that hot shower and stand there with my face feeling that warm water run over me, I not only experience pleasure but have a return of energy. How many times have you relaxed in a tub enjoying the pleasures of that hot bath? It truly is a simple pleasure but life is made up of very simple pleasures. How many times have you said after a hectic day, "I need a hot bath to relax?" Using a hot towel just out of the dryer adds to the completeness of the simple pleasure of that relaxing therapeutic bath.

How about listening to your favorite music? Have you ever sat in your favorite chair with pure quietness in the room, put on that record, close your eyes and just listen to the music? I know I don't hear it for very long, as I fall asleep. But while I was awake it was sheer pleasure.

Then there is the simple pleasure of getting out of bed every morning and being grateful for another beautiful day, maybe not even experiencing aches and pains yet.

Taking a scenic drive is a total pleasure, as we do not have a time clock to watch and we are free to enjoy the beauty of nature that all seasons provide us. As we are driving, we may get hungry and stop and have a meal at some restaurant to which we have never been. It is a different menu prepared by different cooks, but I would say that nine out of ten times, we experience a great meal, especially if it's "down home country cookin'."

How about getting a letter from a friend that you have not heard from in many years? As you read the letter, memories start coming to mind about times you have shared. This happened to me recently and I remembered the terrific luncheons we had together while being assigned on a project that was far from home for both of us. We reminisced about funny stories of things we had done and stories about our families. Today we communicate with one another at least every two months. To me this truly a pleasure.

Is it not a pleasure to have your daughter drop over to the house without advance notice? When ours comes to visit, she may bring along with her some favorite dish or drink and take some time to just sit down to talk and laugh with us. It is wonderful to see how thoughtful our daughter is and to experience the pleasure of the unplanned occasion. It makes our day.

The greatest pleasure that I have today as I enjoy retirement is at dinnertime when I sit with my wife of fifty-six years and enjoy our meal together. Following the meal, we peruse the news and maybe watch a movie. Now it is not all smooth-sailing when it comes to deciding what we are going to watch on TV—sports or movie—but being the nice lady she is, I usually win and she does some reading. However, she does make several appearances, asking when the game will be over. Anyway, the point is she still wants to sit down with me and enjoy a little homemade variety of entertainment—the best of all forms of entertainment, in my opinion.

1960-1969
"Times of Turbulence"

"Peace, peace when there is no peace!" The decade of the sixties was filled with the outcry for peace—peace in Vietnam, peace between generations, peace for those who wanted "to do their own thing." Yet the sixties were, in reality, a great time of turbulence, both in our country, and around the globe. What words come to mind when we think of the turbulent sixties? How about: "flower children;" civil rights; Vietnam; Cuban crisis; Berlin wall. On the lighter side: James Bond; miniskirts; "Sound of Music;" The Beatles. These words reveal much about the mindset of the sixties. The events that occurred in the sixties were, for many, life-changing events. Some were of great historical significance. For instance, in the US there was much disagreement over war issues, chiefly a great backlash among eligible young men trying to avoid the draft. The Vietnam War did not confine its conflict to a small nation across the world from us but within our nation as well as we coped with the war protests coming from the "flower children" and their message of peace, love, and brotherhood. Their mindset was aided by psychotropic drugs, though at that time the long-term affects were unknown. As more information became available, the "war on drugs" began. This nation has not been the same since. The moral fabric of America began to unravel, as young people became cynical about the "Establishment" (people over age 30!). Values were questioned, decisions challenged, and the road toward self-destruction rose up before us.

Certainly there were good things that happened during the sixties also. In the world of medicine, Dr. Barnard perfomed the first heart transplant in 1967. Great technological and scientific progress was made. Neil Armstrong was the first man to walk on the moon! Millions watched on their TV sets as it was happening. The Computer Age was coming into its own, catapulting technology into the last half of the 20th century. The children's TV show called "Sesame Street" began a long career of teaching and influencing our children. The movies "Sound of Music" and "Mary Poppins" entered the scene in 1965.

Most significantly, the traditions and values once held dear by the generations coming out of the Depression, World War II, and the "Happy Days" of the fifties were being tossed aside in favor of "free expression" and a tendency toward irresponsibility. The sixties were indeed a turbulent time in our history and certainly a time of tremendous transition. We are still reeling from the effects today as we embark on a new century.

SECTION 4

CELEBRATIONS AND COMMEMORATIONS

CHAPTER ELEVEN

Happy New Year!

January 1st is a time to evaluate the past year as it relates to health, mistakes that we may have made, and the things we did right. Our future very much depends on our history. With this perspective, we can declare a "statement of direction" for the coming year.

One of the things I do as a senior is to evaluate my health. This evaluation takes the form of questions:

- Did I eat right?
- Did I exercise?
- Did I keep busy with meaningful things?
- Did I tell my loved ones that I loved them?
- Did I show acts of kindness and charity?
- Did I help someone?

We as seniors, as a rule, address these things not only on New Year's Day but also periodically during the year.

The new goals that we set for ourselves should be measurable and obtainable. I feel that we should write these goals down and put them in a place that we can see everyday. The refrigerator serves as a good place because one of our most common goals is to watch what and how much we eat.

New Year's Day celebrations are different according to our age bracket. When I was young and single I went to parties which were held in the school gym, with teachers and parents supervising the festivities. I remember one in particular where we had a "jitterbug" contest. Girls wore the "bobby sox" and the boys wore the "pegged pants."

* * * * *

Historical Moment from 1954
Bill Haley and the Comets are ready to rock up the charts
with their latestrecord, "Rock Around the Clock."
This exciting new sound with a driving rhythm-and-blues
dance beat is already a great hit for the band.
It's called "Rock n' Roll."

* * * * *

As time marched on, I married and had a young family. The New Year's Eve celebrations were celebrated in our homes, as a rule, with family and friends in attendance and the home decorated. I remember there were a lot of traditions, such as eating some "herring and crackers" on New Year's Eve. I really did not relish this tradition but I ate this concoction anyway, but washed it down very quickly.

As the children were growing up and were in High School, it was their time to celebrate. The predominance of High School New Year celebrations in the school gym seemed to have disappeared but the house parties were abundant. Now the challenge for the parents was to indoctrinate the child on the rules of "partying." They always had a curfew and the guys were expected to buy flowers for the girls. The girls started getting ready a week ahead of time. The boys got the car all shined up. And the phone lines became very busy, as this was a major happening. The parents had to call to assure there would be supervision at the party (in a very discreet manner as not to offend). There was a feeling of excitement as they got ready for this happy event.

As we look back, these were great times as we saw the children begin to mature and assume responsibilities, but it took a whole family to assure they did have a safe and happy New Year.

Now the children are gone and there are still the parties for the senior set, but they become more sedate. The big parties are for the most part gone. Celebrations are limited to a few friends or a dance at one of the organizations, and sometimes it is just Mom and Dad sitting watching television, trying with all their might to stay up until midnight and watch the celebration at Times Square in New York. What often happens though is they dose off to "slumberland," letting the very young pick up the baton for the New Year's Eve celebrations.

CHAPTER TWELVE

Valentine's Day

Valentine's Day has been around for hundreds of years. It was in AD 496 that Pope Gelasius I named February 14th as "Valentine's Day." This is not an official holiday but a lot of Americans celebrate this day, from grade school children to senior adults.

Grade school celebration

As I best remember, the celebration at elementary school consisted of bringing of valentines with cute sayings and putting them in a decorated box (representing a mail box) with a slot at the top. This was done during the week and on February the 14th, the children had their party. At the end of the party day, each child would reach in and get a valentine with the contributor's name on the card. Once the valentines had been distributed, they had a small party with refreshments. There was a lot of preparation in getting ready for this day. Again, as I remember, most of the valentines were handmade out of red paper in the shape of a heart. Some very creative youngsters made the card in the form of Cupid with his bow and arrow. I believe the girls were more creative and artistic than the boys.

Love from the Heart

As we reach adulthood, the recognition and exchanging of Valentines becomes more elaborate. It is now a day for sweethearts and friends. It is the day that you show you care. Sending roses (the flower of love) or candy shows this but the Valentine's card is the most popular way of showing your affection.

It is my belief that having a day to recognize your friends and sweethearts is great. It reminds you that love does exist in this day and age. I am sure that during the year we all showed and received all kinds of love and affection in many ways. Today, for example, I was at a senior meeting and was sitting with two gentlemen in their eighties. Both had experienced heart attacks some years ago but they were doing great. As we ate our lunch, we were sharing stories of years gone by and I could see the enthusiasm in their eyes and the smiles on their faces. To me, this was a luncheon where I felt the love of my fellow man.

During the year I am sure that many parents have shown "tough love" to their children by making decisions that their children did not like and they probably even got upset. But you as the parent "stuck to your guns" because you knew what was good for them, even though you may not have been popular at that point in time. This is hard on parents because they really do want to make their children happy. So, parents, take this Valentine's Day opportunity to share your unconditional love with your children.

In conclusion, you might say that Valentine's Day could be called "Hearts' Day," for it offers us a reminder that those near and dear to our hearts are loved and cherished (whether relative or dear friend), and this goes a long way toward helping us overlook the less happy times and focus on the positive things in our relationships.

CHAPTER THIRTEEN

Easter Sunday

E aster is a Christian holiday that celebrates the resurrection of Christ. But as with almost all Christian holidays, Easter has been and continues to be secularized and commercialized more and more.

As a child growing up in the '30s and '40s, I can remember the families getting dressed up in their finest to go to church to celebrate the Christian tradition of the history-changing resurrection of Jesus Christ.

After celebrating with wonderful uplifting music and worshipping together, we would have Easter egg hunts on the church grounds, followed up by the families getting together for a lavish meal. It was very simple and not a lot of expense was incurred for fancy clothes or gifts. This was due to its being in a farm community. We did not have department stores with the finest of clothes and those fine hats, nor could we have afforded them had they been available. We could not eat the clothes but could buy seed to grow the food for the table. I guess you might say that fancy clothes were not a priority.

Chickens were plentiful, therefore having enough eggs for the hunt was no problem. As a side note, I remember my grandmother would sell eggs to a man from town who in turn sold them to the grocery store. This was a way that she would earn "pin" money for store-bought items she might want to buy on her trip to town.

The coloring of eggs was a family affair. Everyone gathered around the huge kitchen table and went to work coloring the eggs. Artistic pride was at stake. Coloring of the eggs was a thought process that involved coming up with a particular design. Now several adults of the family hid the eggs on Easter Sunday, early in the morning to assure no potential searchers made early discoveries. The egg hunt took place after the major dinner ("lunch" as we call it today and what we call "dinner" today was then known as "supper"). The size of families was huge in those days so there was always a crowd.

The dinners were great and, as I remember, the main meat was ham. The "fixin's" were also great. We had everything imaginable. I remember the cellars where the canned fruits and vegetables were kept in those Mason jars that were sealed with a wax coating on the top. After dinner, the adults talked, the children played games, and we all topped the day off with homemade ice cream.

Today, the tradition of having Easter egg hunts continues, but more than that, it is a special day of worship for those who believe in the resurrection of Jesus Christ. It is also a day of family get-togethers, large dinners (still ham as the main dish), and when all the festivities are over, a time of reflection on the meaning of Easter for our lives.

CHAPTER FOURTEEN

Mother's Day

It is my understanding that Mother's Day is the busiest day for the restaurant business—

the reason being that Mom has been the one who has made all those meals during the year and this day she will not only be honored but be served. I guess one can conclude that Dad is not the best of cooks, but maybe the holiday also gives us opportunity to take not only Mom out to lunch or dinner but also the grandmothers and, in some cases, the great-grandmothers. Of course this means the fathers, grandfathers, and great-grandfathers are included. This has now grown into a sizable group at the restaurant and it would definitely be a challenge for Dad to create this feast at home.

If you really think about it, Mom is the centerpiece of the family. She is the one who has the patience and understanding and she is the one who takes time to be a good listener, regardless of how busy she is and how poorly she may be feeling at that given point. You can see the compassion in her eyes and hear it in her tone of voice.

Now some of today's moms, in addition to being the homemakers, have taken on an additional workload at a job outside the home, either part-time or full-time. This is a lot different from when I was a child growing up in the '30s and '40s when the majority of the moms stayed home, engaging in that most important of jobs, taking care of the family and home.

It is my viewpoint that moms are moms, regardless if they are the "grand" moms or "great-grand" moms. Their roles are relative to the pecking order in the family unit as sometimes the grand- and even great-grandmoms are all called to active duty to fill in for a mom who is absent for some reason. This is how it should be in a family. I feel that this happens more frequently today than in years past due to the prevalence of so-called "working moms." Actually, they're all working moms—it's just that some work in the home and some outside home.

I remember my grandmother who was always there for me, filling in the duties of my mom. She was the enforcer when it came to scrubbing behind my ears, filling the wood box, reading a chapter in the Bible, saying my prayers and getting to bed on time. In addition, she was the nurse who put medicine on my cuts, the teacher's helper who reviewed my home work, the seamstress who patched my clothes, and the fashion coordinator who made sure I did not have a "cowlick" on the back of my head before I went to school. As a youngster, I helped her in the "truck garden" growing vegetables for our table. She not only was my grandmother but she was my friend and I owe her for the solid foundation she gave me as a young boy.

Time marches on and now I see firsthand another mom whom I have known for over fifty-six years. To this day, after four children, seven grandchildren and five great-grandchildren, she is still a mom. What duties do I see her perform? She has true concern for each member of the family, even in the early hours of the morning if someone is sick. She continues to be on call for baby-sitting duties. She is in attendance at all births. Her house still maintains dolls and toys for the visits by the children. Everybody is remembered on the holidays and the list could go on and on. The main thing that endears her to all is not the material gifts she gives but rather the love and heart of a mom. I have the privilege of seeing this everyday, as this describes my wife. In addition, I see other grandmothers being called on to fill in as moms for their own grandchildren. My point is that mothers never relinquish the title of "Mom," regardless of age.

I believe that moms will continue the tradition of being the loving listener, caring, patient enforcer and spiritual leader of the family because they were taught by the "very best"— the "grand" and "great-grand" moms.

CHAPTER FIFTEEN

Armed Forces Day/Memorial Day

Armed Forces Day

According to a New York Times article published on May 17, 1952:

> This is the day on which we have the welcome opportunity to pay special tribute to the men and women of the Armed Forces ... to all the individuals who are in the service of their country all over the world. Armed Forces Day won't be a matter of parades and receptions for a good many of them. They will all be in line of duty and some of them may give their lives in that duty.

How ironic that these words were being said in 1952 and now, some 52 years later, our service men and women are again in "harm's way" for the specific purpose of fighting in the War on Terrorism, resulting in the protection of our freedoms.

The Unification Bill was passed in 1947. It created the

Department of Defense and replaced the Office of the Secretary of War with that of the Secretary of Defense. Then Secretary Stimson considered this as the most important peacetime reform in our military history. He later wrote,

> Under a single leader, the Army, the Navy and the Air Forces could now learn, and be taught, to live together. The great gains of World War Two might thus be consolidated, while a repetition of its occasional failures could be prevented.[88]

On August 31, 1949, Secretary of Defense Louis Johnson announced the creation of an Armed Forces Day to replace separate Army, Navy and Air Force Days. The single-day celebration stemmed from the unification of the Armed Forces under one department— the Department of Defense.

On this day we should be grateful for the members of the armed services as they put their lives on the line to protect those freedoms that we enjoy. This includes freedoms that some of us believe are way out of bounds, such as the debate by some on the inclusion of "under God" in our Pledge of Allegiance.

As I write this, I see every evening on television our service people being interviewed by the imbedded correspondents in Iraq. I am sure that we are all so proud to hear those young people express themselves in ways that are truly American and patriotic. It gives me goose bumps just to listen to them.

You can see the unity of all the services (which was the goal of the Unification Bill) in the coordination and communication among all branches of service. The modernization of logistics has resulted in an outstanding achievement that we have witnessed by the achievements in the Gulf War and in Operation Iraqi Freedom, as we have been made aware of the timely availability of supplies and personnel in support of the military plans. (I say, "Atta boy.") This logistics support is a major player in the ability to achieve the objectives of the plan. Again, taking into consideration the logistics challenge with all the factors such as the services' roles, the demographics and the hundreds of thousands of personnel and equipment, this is a major success for our Armed Services. I might note that the plan of getting equipment and personnel into Iraq was changed when Turkey did not allow our troops to come in from the north. Even at that, our military leaders "improvised" and the plan was still a success.

Let's remember on this Armed Services Day that the relative peace—as the enemy is not walking down our main streets and we are not under siege—and achievements in war are a result of the sacrifices of those in our Armed Services. It is as simple as that.

We salute the brave men and women who are following in the footsteps and traditions of our Armed Forces of days gone by and now continue to protect our country, defend our freedoms, and help make our world a better place in which to live. God bless our Armed Services and keep them out of harm's way.

Memorial Day

This day was initiated in memory of our honored dead. This day now includes those Armed Services members who are missing in action (MIA). This day—which has a history going back to the civil war—is much more than a three-day weekend that marks the beginning of summer. To veterans and families who have lost love ones in service to our country, it is a reminder of those who died so that we can enjoy the freedoms we have today.

In my senior generation group we have seen many wars and some have experienced the horrific sights of death while serving our country. I am sure these brave veterans have vivid memories of the loss of their comrades, no matter how long ago it occurred. To give a perspective on the magnitude of loss of life to preserve our freedoms, the following are some approximate figures dealing with the American Armed Services in wartime:

- World War II – over 400,000
- Korean War – over 54,000
- Vietnam War – over 100,000
- Persian Gulf War – 148
- Ongoing wars in Afghanistan and Iraq – several hundreds of

casualties at this point in time.

Memorial Day weekend is a time when we see volunteers selling the small red artificial roses as a fundraiser for our disabled veterans. It is a time when the custom of placing flowers and small flags on the graves of those who have fallen in combat. If you live in Missouri and have never visited Jefferson Barracks on this day of recognition, you should take that drive and see the awesome view. While you are there, have a moment of silence, remembering our fallen soldiers. If you live elsewhere, I encourage you to visit whatever local veteran's memorial available in your area. Let us also not forget about the many graves of those who died for our freedom that are on foreign soil, such as those from World War II who are buried in France.

This is a day of family picnics or get-togethers, so this is an opportune time to tell our children the true meaning of this day. Along with the moms and dads, I am sure the grandparents will agree on the significance of this day. It is my view that one of the most important responsibilities that we have as members of a free-born society is to transmit that freedom to the children. In addition to the memorial to our honored dead and those still missing in action, one cannot help but think about their families who are left with these sad memories. I remember so vividly the families that received telegrams in World War II, the Korean War and Vietnam. I remember one of the first families in my town of Florissant receiving the telegram telling of the loss of their only son in the Vietnam War. What a sorrowful time when this happens for family and friends. So, on this Memorial Day, let's remember their heroism and think back to the happy times we shared with these "beautiful people," as they are true heroes.

* * * * *

Eulogy for a Veteran

Do not stand at my grave and weep.

I am not there, I do not sleep.

I am a thousand winds that blow.

I am the diamond glints on snow.

I am the sunlight on ripened grain.

I am the gentle autumn rain.

When you awaken in the morning's hush,

I am the swift uplifting rush

of quiet birds in circled flight,

I am the soft stars that shine at night.

Do not stand at my grave and cry,

I am not there, I did not die.

(Author Unknown)

* * * * *

CHAPTER SIXTEEN

Fourth of July – Independence Day

"I pledge allegiance to the flag of the United States of America and to the Republic for which it stands, one Nation under God, indivisible, with liberty and justice for all."

In our most recent times there have been some questions by some about the use of these words "one Nation under God." In addition, the saying of the Pledge of Allegiance to the Flag in public schools prior to the starting of the school day has been challenged. Well, I just want to say that this country was founded on such words, backed by the spirit of those words. Therefore, why are these words questioned? I guess it is just another case of political correctness by some.

On July 4th, 1776, we claimed our independence from England and democracy for America was born. So, as a refresher course, I am including the words here to remind us all what "the real reason" is behind the celebration of July the 4th. So please read the words of our United States Declaration of Independence very carefully.

We hold these truths to be self-evident, that all men are created equal, that they are endowed by their Creator with certain unalienable Rights, that among these are Life, Liberty, and the pursuit of Happiness. That to secure these rights, Governments are instituted among Men, deriving their just powers from the consent of the governed. That whenever any Form of Government becomes destructive of these ends, it is the Right of the People to alter or to abolish it, and to institute new Government, laying its foundation on such principles and organizing its powers in such form, as to them shall seem most likely to effect their Safety and Happiness.

There were many intolerable actions by King George III of Great Britain that caused this declaration to arise from what was then known as The Colonies. One that stands out to me and, in my opinion, we are faced with today as well, was the fact that taxes were imposed on us without our consent. I believe that we are being over-taxed today, even though we supposedly have a representative form of government. For example, I have never been questioned by any of my representatives on how they should vote relative to legislation regarding taxes. I believe that government should be run as a business, with responsibility and wise stewardship (more on taxes in Section 3).

The 4th of July has great significance for the people of the United States, and we must from time to time think about how we got to where we are today. In addition, let's remember our Armed Services and other personnel involved in reconnaissance operations who have died in order that we may continue to live according to the spirit of the "Declaration of Independence." This document serves as a model to the world, and we see this fact in the thousands who leave their homeland every day to *legally* come to the "land of the free and the home of the brave" so they can begin living their American Dream.

Each year on July 4th, Americans celebrate that freedom and independence with barbecues, picnics, and family gatherings. Cities have bands and fireworks displays and the spirit of freedom, allegiance to and pride in being an American, are ever present. When we sing songs like "America" ("My country 'tis of thee"), "America the Beautiful," "The Star Spangled Banner," "Yankee Doodle Dandy" and, for you veterans, the songs that represent each branch of service, let's get those "goose bumps" back on our arms.

On July 4th 1776, The Declaration of Independence was a revolutionary step in a process of defining how people should govern themselves for the good of the individual as well as society. Thanks to our forefathers and foremothers, we have the freedoms to vote, complain, speak, worship, be creative, to invest in one's future and so many more freedoms that we all take for granted.

Let us examine this phrase: "Deriving their just powers from the people." That means we must take an interest in our elected officials who represent our will. They are there to serve us, the people. They are not there to promote their agenda or personal political ambitions, but to do our bidding. If they do not support the wishes of the majority of their constituents—vote them out and elect someone who will. But in order to do that, you must keep informed and then vote.

I know that Flag Day is not celebrated much in our country, but I feel that the flag embodies the essence of freedom and is really a part of the 4th of July celebration. It represents the spirit of the American nation and the history of the American people. It symbolizes the success of a government of and for the people, civic and religious freedoms and a country blessed with natural resources. Congress first authorized the flag June 14, 1777. This past Flag Day, as I drove through my neighborhood, I could count on one hand the number of flags on display. I mention this so that when we celebrate Flag Day and 4th of July, let's have private homes and places of business displaying our proud American flag, showing that we are proud to be Americans.

When the Declaration of Independence was declared, John Adams wrote this historic letter to his wife:

> I am apt to believe that this day will be celebrated by succeeding generations as the great anniversary festival. It ought to be commemorated as the day of deliverance, by solemn acts of devotion to God almighty. It ought to be

solemnized with pomp and parade, with shows, games, sports, guns, bells, bonfires, and illuminations, from one end of this continent to the other, from this time forward forevermore.[98]

Just think of the foresight and wisdom with which our founding fathers were blessed. In addition, think of the personal scarifices they made in order for us to celebrate this holiday of Independence Day.

Finally, I want to urge us to remind the younger generation what this holiday is really all about, prior to enjoying the celebrations. I feel it would be great to do this—maybe read them the Declaration of Independence and explain to them the greatness and wisdom of those people who put this document together so many years ago. To me it is amazing what they accomplished. This is the foundation for our great country—God Bless America!

More on the "Good Old USA"

I want to take a moment to reflect a little more on how blessed we are to be living in this country of ours. We as families have been blessed with the freedoms of choice regarding education, religion, medical care, speech, voting, where we live, chosen profession and many other freedoms too numerous to count. This means that we have the opportunity to determine the environment in which to raise children, preparing them to become responsible persons as well as good citizens.

For those of us who are considered seniors now, we were brought up in a nation in which our enemies were identifiable. We had the Axis powers of Europe, the North Koreans, Communist Vietnamese, the Iraqis of the Gulf War. We knew who they were for the most part.

Many people have given their lives in order that we may continue to enjoy these freedoms and I am sure there will continue to be sacrifices made in order to maintain these freedoms. Our lives have already changed with the new threat to our freedoms called terrorism. We have been forced to come up with a way to fight this new enemy. We have increased security at all critical points of transportation, energy sites, many public buildings, the assembly of large groups of people, major celebrations, sporting events and the list goes on and on. We have laws for immigration, student visas, investigations, communications and so much more, with the objective of protecting our freedoms. Our Armed Forces and agents are scattered to all parts of the world. Some we hear about, but many others are working behind the scenes in the attempt to stop terrorist activity, both here and abroad.

One thing about Americans that I have learned over a lifetime is our ability to "rise to the occasion." We know how to unite and produce whatever weapons are needed to fight our enemies. As a nation, we place great value on the individual, and we all hurt when even a few are attacked from without. Again, we have compassion for the hurting, as evidenced by the outpouring of love in the aftermath of the 9/11 tragedy. Hidden in our hearts is the objective to protect our land, people and freedoms.

That is why I must say that we are truly blessed to be living in a land of freedom. We have the ability to join together of our own free will to fight our enemies. There are many ways that we do this such as: being in the Armed Services and law enforcement, working as firemen, working in manufacturing plants and in the scientific and medical fields, and so many other professions. There is also a spirit of patriotism that makes us proud to be Americans. But the one thing that makes this all happen, in my opinion, is prayer and believing in God. It was quite evident by the surge in church attendance and public prayer that followed the World Trade Center tragedy that though it may appear at times that we don't care about expressing our faith, when it comes down to fundamentals, we know we must trust God when things are out of control. We must continue in faith and prayer, teaching our children that not only are we to be good citizens, but our freedoms are worth fighting for. May our country continue to be blessed and be a blessing in the world.

Today we hear so many stories about eliminating any public phrase, statement, or expression that uses the word "God." In addition, the display of the Ten Commandments on public property is being protested. It is really hard for me to understand this assault on one of the foundational stones laid by our forefathers.

We need to respect what was written in stone many decades ago at a time when this country believed in the public display of phrases, statements and expressions with the word "God" and the Ten Commandments.

Remember that:

- Since 1777, a prayer has been offered prior to opening up a session of Congress.
- The founders of the Constitution of the United States of America were all members of orthodox churches.
- Patrick Henry said the following, "It cannot be emphasized too strongly or too often that this great nation was not founded not by religionists but by Christians, not on religions but on the Gospel of Jesus Christ."[106]
- The fourth president of the United States, James Madison, in addition to being called "The Father of the Constitution," made the following statement: "We have staked the whole of all our political institutions upon the capacity of mankind for self government, upon the capacity of each and all of us to govern ourselves, to control ourselves, to sustain ourselves according to the Ten Commandments of God."[117]

The building in Washington DC that houses the Supreme Court and those who try the laws of the land is symbolic of what our forefathers deemed important as the foundation of and the preservation of our freedoms. This building has many displays of what the foundation of this country was built on, for example:

- Depicted on the front of the building, there is a row of lawmakers facing one person in the middle (who is facing forward with a full frontal view). This person just happens to be Moses, who is holding the tablets containing the Ten Commandments.
- Inside the courtroom, displayed on the wall behind and above where the judges sit, there is a display of the Ten Commandments.
- As you visit Washington DC, please take note of Bible verses etched all over the federal buildings and monuments.

So it is hard to understand the assault on our country's foundation, which has stood for several hundred years. It is the "rock" that makes this the greatest country on the earth.

We are a country of diversity, with many religious beliefs, ethnic customs and philosophical views. We must be able to afford the rights to every citizen but not at the price of discounting our own unique American heritage.

* * * * *

Historical Moment from 1980
Ronald Reagan (age 69) defeated incumbent Jimmy Carter
in a landslide victory and became our new president.

* * * * *

CHAPTER SEVENTEEN

Veteran's Day

For the Veteran's Day holiday,
I offer these tributes by unknown authors:

* * * * *

God Bless Them

It is the VETERAN, not the preacher,
who has given us freedom of religion.
It is the VETERAN, not the reporter,
who has given us freedom of the press.
It is the VETERAN, not the poet,
who has given us freedom of speech.
It is the VETERAN, not the campus organizer,
who has given us freedom to assemble.
It is the VETERAN, not the lawyer,
who has given us the right to a fair trial.
It is the VETERAN, not the politician,
Who has given us the right to vote.

* * * * *

* * * * *

Veterans

On the ABC evening news in the fall of 2003 it was reported that, because of the dangers from Hurricane Isabelle approaching Washington DC, the military members assigned the duty of guarding the Tomb of the Unknown Soldier were given permission to suspend the assignment.

They refused. "No way, Sir!"

Soaked to the skin, marching in the pelting rain of a tropical storm, they said that guarding the Tomb was not just an assignment, it was the highest honor that can be afforded to a service person.

The tomb has been patrolled continuously, 24/7, since 1930. We can be very proud of our young men and women in the service no matter where they serve.

* * * * *

CHAPTER EIGHTEEN

Thanksgiving

Thanksgiving: "Throughout the United States ...Thanksgiving Day is an annual legal holiday. It is celebrated on the fourth Thursday in November...The American holiday commemorates a harvest celebration held by the Pilgrims of Plymouth colony in 1621."[129] Prior to the Thanksgiving celebrations here in America, the Western Europeans celebrated "Harvest Home Festivals" for the successful completion of "bringing in the crops." Thanksgiving was first celebrated in America by the Pilgrims (early English settlers) and the Native Americans in Colonial New England in the early 1 7th century.

What a blessing to live in a country where we have established one day out of the year to give thanks. And we do have so many things for which to be thankful. This book states my opinions about the decline of morality in our society. It is truly a blessing to be able to freely state my opinions for the public to read, regardless if they agree with me or not.

Freedom to worship is something that so many people around the world do not have. In fact, as you read this, there is on-going religious persecution in many other countries. What a shame! Try to imagine getting ready to worship with the fear that someone would intrude and punish you on the spot or take you off to a prison or like confinement. It is hard to believe that this is still happening in many places in the world, but it is.

We are free to elect our government representatives who make our rules, laws and government regulations. It seems to me that this freedom is one that is greatly neglected and it is so hard to understand why this is the case. Think about it! These laws and regulations have an impact on our daily living. Look at the number of countries that do not have free elections and where tyranny rules. Look at the countries of the world where violent coups are the norm. With this perspective, we should desire to exercise our freedom to elect our representatives—yes, they are put there to do our bidding as they work for us, their constituents. In this way, we can have a voice in maintaining our freedoms that we celebrate on Thanksgiving Day.

For the most part, the economic environment of our country is one of potential prosperity and unlimited opportunity for all of its citizens. Let us give thanks on Thanksgiving Day for this wonderful blessing.

From my viewpoint, when you say the word "Thanksgiving" (referring to the holiday), the following images come to mind. Sometimes it is cold outside with the entire family in the house talking, getting the meal ready, watching football on television. The windows are frosted due to the warmth in the house and cold outside. There are Thanksgivings with snow on the ground and love in the air. Most of all, it is a gathering time for family and friends, which is so important in life.

Finally, the main event of the gathering is about to begin—mealtime. Someone says the prayer and now it is time to "chow down." What a meal! Everything imaginable is there for one to satisfy his taste buds. Talking is predominant, with the added noise of the clinking of dishes and utensils. The eating continues regardless of diet plans and sometimes other controlling factors. The main course is done and now it is time for dessert. Pies, fruit, ice cream and other delights appear before us. Now the official mealtime is done and the focus is on football or, for those not into football, there are conversations throughout the house from the kitchen to the dining room to the large room. This is quality time for family and friends. You see periodic visits to the kitchen to get a piece of turkey or dessert as we just can't get enough of that delicious meal. Now it is time to go our various ways and the host is packing some food for the departing guests out of the great abundance of culinary delights. The day is done and another wonderful Thanksgiving Day has passed into the family's book of memories. Thanksgiving is truly a celebration of domestic life centered on the home and family.

So nothing really has changed from the "olden days," except some of the family members that used to be the ones playing childish games have now brought their children to the feast. The older members who had to prepare the meals and do the planning in the past have turned those duties over to their daughters and daughters-in-law and they themselves have become the "official food consultants." The football games are basically the same except for the uniforms, technology, and all of the experts talking during the game at half-time. We are told what the teams are doing wrong and what they have to do to win.

We now engage in picture-taking, using camcorders, digital cameras and other equipment, unlike Thanksgivings of the past when we had Kodak box cameras. Those having the digital cameras are now able to put them on the family web page to see and enjoy for those members that have access to computers. There goes the traditional family album!

* * * * *

Historical Tidbit from 1948
American inventor Edwin Land has created a camera that can develop and print its own photographs—within one minute of taking the picture. The Polaroid Land camera weights 5 lbs (2.25kg) and costs $95.

* * * * *

The food that is served today is, as I remember, the same dishes that we had in an era gone by. Today, though, the vegetables come from the freezer and microwave ovens, and George Forman grills are used in the cooking. The feast includes vegetables, desserts, the traditional turkey and dressing (which the food consultants always prepare, bringing their magic to that dish that accompanies the bird) and the homemade mashed potatoes.

The one common thread that brings the events of this day together is called love. Love of family has been consistent through time and will always be as far as I am concerned. Maybe this day of thanksgiving is not only for our freedoms but a day of thanksgiving for family—a family focused on love for one another and, in some cases, our very special friends. A day of togetherness rekindles our family unity that will last throughout the coming year as we go back to our day-to-day living.

Thanksgiving is the day in which we must always remember the purpose of the holiday. We take time to acknowledge the blessing of living in a country that is free. One of the main blessings that we enjoy as citizens of the United States is the freedom to worship. This freedom is at the very core of our country's declaration of independence from England, a church state. Let us give thanks for this freedom especially. This truly is a day to take a moment and realize that all our blessings and freedoms come from God. Let us recognize Him as the Source.

CHAPTER NINETEEN

Pearl Harbor Day

Today there is not usually much recognition for December 7th —Pearl Harbor Day. Many times on this date I have asked many middle-aged and younger people what event in history happened on this date and they did not know. Am I expecting too much? I don't think so. I hope that the history books in our schools are educating the children on the significance of what happened on this date, especially since a lot of the living grandparents of the children in the classes lived through this period. Sometimes you have to look into the past to see your future. This is not only true for individuals but also nations. In the business arena I have been on projects where one of the key tasks was to make is a "lessons learned" data file. Why? So other people in the company would not make the same mistake. Parents and grandparents sometimes are portrayed as so wise because they've "been there/done that," as the young people would say. So when we seniors have the chance to tell our stories, let's tell them about Pearl Harbor and the many sacrifices and heroes of that generation.

Pearl Harbor was the site of a surprise attack on the United States by Japanese military forces on December 7, 1941. Japanese ships and airplanes attacked the United States naval base at Pearl Harbor on the island of Oahu in Hawaii. Military personnel were at church or enjoying family life on the beautiful Islands. The attack caused heavy casualties and destroyed much of the American Pacific Fleet. The attack also brought the United States into World War II. "Remember Pearl Harbor" became the rallying cry for the country. I remember another phrase that came from this event—"a sneak attack." American participation was a crucial reason why the embattled Allied nations, including the United Kingdom (UK) and Soviet Union, turned the tide and defeated the Axis nations, headed by Japan and Germany. There had been much discussion within the United States as to whether or not we should enter the war in Europe, but this heinous act leveled against us left no doubt. Another famous phrase that we seniors remember is what President Roosevelt termed December 7th —"a date which will live in infamy." I must say the nation rallied. President Roosevelt declared war on December 8th, without any discussion by Congress, and the war effort began. Enlistment into the service and plans for preparing a military buildup began. Major corporations joined in with the planning and got rid of the trucks with the sign on the side saying "tank."

Basic training for some of the older soldiers was rough, even to the point their feet bled due to the extensive marching and calisthenics. Jefferson Barracks near where I lived at the time was totally mobilized, as I'm sure were most of the military bases around the country. As the war progressed and we started taking German prisoners of war, some of us local folks found full time employment in the base laundry at Jefferson Barracks.

I don't know if what I am about to write is politically correct, but I am going to do it anyway. I have the impression that our young people of today really don't know how horrible this war was, not only for the military, but the families who were left behind not knowing the well-being of their loved ones. A recent movie ("*Pearl Harbor*") was made and presented to movie-going audiences. But, in my opinion, it was done in such a way as to be "politically correct." The point I want to make is that when we tell, teach and learn about our country's history, it should be honest and forthright. Note: it is my opinion that another movie entitled "*Black Hawk Down*" did not tell the whole story, forgetting the political background of this disaster. Tell it as it is.

So let's all have a moment of remembrance for this "date which will live in infamy," a date that brought us into another world war. Many lives were lost to save our country and retain all of our freedoms that we sometimes take for granted. "Remember Pearl Harbor!"

CHAPTER TWENTY

Christmas

Christmas is a Christian holiday that celebrates the birth of Jesus Christ. The word Christmas comes from "Cristes maesse," an early English phrase that means "Mass of Christ."[131]0 The shortened form of the word, Xmas, is sometimes used instead of Christmas. This tradition began early in the Christian church. In Greek, X is the first letter of Christ's name and is frequently used as a holy symbol.

I want to address the memories evoked by some of us who grew up in the '30s and '40s. Christmas was made up of two main ingredients—church and family. It was not a period of time between Thanksgiving and Christmas Eve of frantic shopping, which I feel today is the predominant meaning of Christmas. Today, companies manufacture ornaments, lights, and other seasonal products throughout the year. It has become one of the thermometers as to how the economy is doing. This attention to consumerism is overshadowing the true meaning of Christmas. Materialism—an over abundance of gift giving—cannot replace personal attention given to your loved ones.

A Brown Bag Christmas

This is my Christmas story, and I know that you, my readers, also have similar wonderful memories. I remember this one Christmas Eve in particular that could have been taken out of the movie "It's a Wonderful Life," starring Jimmy Stewart and Donna Reed. The night was so clear and bright and the ground was covered by a fresh snowfall that had not been disturbed by any human or creature. The family was all cleaned up and we walked together on our way to a small country church. Again, the clearness of night, the stars shining so bright, the sound of the snow breaking up as we brought our feet to the ground, the coldness on our faces making it feel so clean and fresh made it a very meaningful walk. The quietness was almost deafening.

As we entered the church, we were blinded with the brightness of the lights that lit up the building. Now you must remember at that point in time of my childhood, we were still using oil lamps in our home to brighten the rooms. When I say brighten the rooms, I mean there were just a few lamps and as we left the central focal point of the home, which was the kitchen, we used the lamp to find our way to our rooms. This lamp also provided the dim light in order to read a chapter of the Bible every night prior to going to bed. The church lights themselves were startling and there in the corner was a huge tree the men had cut down from the forest nearby. There were no tree lots or fully decorated trees in the stores to buy. The decorations were very simple—popcorn strung together, paper loops intertwined to make a chain that covered the tree from top to bottom, candy canes, and religious ornaments, and at the top of the tree, a gigantic star. Large brown bags surrounded the bottom of the tree and we, the children, were very curious of their contents. The service began and even today I can remember the singing. It was loud—no, I think it was thunderous—to my small ears. We all had songbooks and found joy in this time of celebration. Prayer was periodically interjected into the service and I remember being so tuned in to the true meaning of Christmas. When the service was over—which covered several hours of celebration—the children were asked to form a line and come up to the front of the church to get that mysterious "brown bag."

The brown bag was drawn to my chest and I returned to my family, not looking in the bag yet. We then left the church and greeted all of our friends and finally started the walk home with a heart of sheer happiness and, I must say, a sense of internal peace.

We entered our home and shed our winter togs. Boots went by the wooden stove to dry out—they had been rubbed down with linseed oil to protect them from getting water-logged—and now was the time to look into the brown bag. The whole family got around the kitchen table and I opened the bag. The bag was filled with walnuts, pecans, candy canes, apples, oranges and other types of fruits. Now one might say, "Is that all there was?" My answer is, "Yes, that was all there was." But I honestly must say that this was one of the most memorable Christmas celebrations that I experienced as a child. My point is that it was the whole Christmas evening—the snow, the clearness of night, the cold on my face, the church service, the ever present love and friendship—was my Christmas gift. Why? Because I felt the closeness to God, which in my opinion is what Christmas is all about.

1970-1979
"Kaleidoscope Years"

Unlike the other decades of the twentieth century, there is not a defining word or phrase to describe the seventies. There had been the "Roaring Twenties," "The Fabulous Fifties," and the "Turbulent Sixties." The 70s mostly were just an extension of the 60s— more war in Vietnam; more inventions in the growing computer industry; more social unrest among the young; more space exploration. The 1970s saw an ebbing of confidence in the developed world. The sudden rise of oil prices in 1973 disrupted international trade and brought about the return of widespread unemployment. But it was also a decade of progress. The US and the USSR agreed on nuclear weapons reductions. The Space Shuttle, a reusable spacecraft, was built, and the first "test-tube baby" was born (I question whether this was progress!) There grew a heightened awareness of our earth's limited resources, and the war against pollution began in earnest. The "feminist" cause was espoused by women who challenged the traditional roles assigned to them by society. They fought for "sexual and economic freedom and equality."

In contrast to much of the negative focus in real life, the entertainment industry gave us the movie "Love Story," "Jesus Christ Superstar," and DisneyWorld. The voting age was lowered to eighteen. More and more, teenagers became a subculture of consumers. They became the primary purchasers of recorded music and the new "rock video." However, toward the end of the decade, the music would turn angry as the "punk" bands entered the scene and rap music was introduced.

Disenchantment with the government began to grow because we were betrayed by our nation's leaders—namely Richard Nixon and the Watergate Scandal in 1974. Medical breakthroughs included the US Surgeon-general's published report on the cancerous effects of cigarette-smoking. This led to further studies that would demonstrate other deadly diseases were also caused by tobacco.

The erosion of our traditional values that began in the '60s became full-blown rebellion in the '70s. As the younger generation was influenced by the high-profile leaders of this rebellion, respect for people over age 30 was fast becoming a thing of the past.

SECTION 5

INHERITED ATTITUDES

CHAPTER TWENTY-ONE

Attitude toward Life

The definition of attitude is: "a complex mental state involving beliefs and feelings and values and dispositions to act in certain ways." This pretty well covers all aspects of life, does it not? There are two types of attitude—positive and negative. These are the choices we have. I don't think that we really can sit on the fence, as our inner selves will not allow us to do that.

Attitude toward Self

There are attitudes that you have toward yourself and attitudes toward others. You will be better equipped to have a positive attitude toward others if you first think positive thoughts about yourself. You are a human being created by God with a purpose for living. When you realize this, you will begin to see how this influences your actions toward others. It is easy to see this truth in the parent/child relationship. From a parental standpoint, you can influence the attitudes of your children. Attitudes are infectious by nature and I'm sure all of us want our children and grandchildren to be "infected" with positive attitudes.

Attitude and Children

A positive attitude towards your fellow man creates a community spirit that ultimately reaches the nation. I remember years ago when I coached little league baseball teams, that each team seemed to have its own personality that reflected the manager's attitude about the game. The manager who was always hollering at the umpire and was continually being upset by everybody and everything (if he was not winning) was mimicked by the team members. The other kind of manager was very soft-spoken and, if he did have a disagreement with the umpires (who were not much older than the players), he would privately discuss the play on the field. The young players sat calmly on the bench, watching the next batter wait for his turn at bat. The batboy always had the bats and equipment placed in their proper place and so forth. The young players, without realizing it, were getting a lesson in having a positive attitude. They were learning sportsmanship, an attitude that not only concerned the rules of the game and the authority of the coaches and umpires, but also an attitude of respect for their fellow team members. With an attitude of good sportsmanship and respect for others, the game was more enjoyable for all.

Attitude at Work

The attitude you have concerning your job is a key to whether or not you will be happy there as well as whether or not you will work there for very long. I don't know how many times I have heard from managers who state, "Give me an employee who is average but has a good attitude any day versus the intellect who has a negative attitude." The kind of employee a manager wants has an open mind and teachable spirit and team player mentality. If the attitude exhibited at work is more one of "we" rather than "me," the other employees will quickly notice, and so will the management.

In listening to sports managers talk about their winning teams, you may notice that they often refer more to the team members' attitudes than they do about each individual's playing statistics. Coaches, sportscasters, and fans alike want to see team members who get along with each other and are willing to sacrifice their individual goals in order for the team to win. With this kind of attitude displayed by the players, all are winners, regardless of the score.

Attitude about Health

The attitude that you have about your health problems determines to a great extent how your health is managed and whether or not you improve. You must have a positive attitude. For example, let's say your doctor states that you must reduce your weight and give up the "goodies" in order to continue to enjoy good health or to improve an existing health condition. Usually, we get an attitude of "Poor me!" and "Why do I have to do this now?" Well! You have to develop a mental discipline to accomplish this health objective. It won't be easy but you know that with a positive attitude and following the doctor's orders you will see the benefits of losing weight and feeling good about yourself. You will no longer be afraid to get on the scales but are now looking forward to it. What a day when you are able to cross your legs and tie your shoes, when you are able to buy clothes that are not always army green (for men), but be able to get those colored outfits! I suppose you can guess that this has happened to me. I know whereof I speak.

These are just a few of the ways that your attitude affects your life, as well as the lives of others. In this section, we will look at some specific attitudes and their far-reaching consequences.

CHAPTER TWENTY-TWO

Seniors' Perspective on Values

J ust recently, upon the completion of one of my speeches at a senior organization meeting, a senior said to me that we need more people spreading the word concerning the decline of societal values in our country. By spreading the word we will help reverse this trend toward of social decline. Again, some will say, "How can little old me make a difference?" Well, the answer to that if all the "little old me's" are added up, they will make a difference. An analogy of this goes back to World War II. We urgently needed the planes and ammunition to defeat the Axis powers. When we were attacked, we were not prepared. It was the American work force made up of the "little old me's" (symbolized by Rosie the Riveter) that became juggernauts in production of war goods. Hence we were able to the defeat the enemy.

Now how do we, as seniors, become juggernauts in influencing a change of direction for our country as it relates to social decline? How can we stem the tide of immorality, obscenity in our entertainment industry in all venues, including television, movies, the Internet, books and magazines? Finally, how can we stem the tide regarding individual actions that lead to crime on the streets and in the workplace?

Respect

Before we answer these questions, we must first ask, "What makes seniors experts on this subject matter?" Well, I'm glad you asked. We grew up in era when we had a high standard of social values. Remember back in the '30s and '40s when we went to school and the teacher asked a question? You stood up and respectfully answered the question and always addressed the teacher by the appropriate salutation. When you addressed relatives, you again addressed them by the proper salutation such as Uncle, Aunt, etc. This to me is a sign of respect.

We come from an era when the family unit consisted of Mom, Dad and the kids, all living under one roof called "home." We had our definite roles, with Dad earning the household income and Mom taking care of the home. A traditional family scene was when everyone ate dinner (supper) together. Typically, children were disciplined with a whipping on the "bottom" as required, without the fear of being sued. The whole family went to school events together, enjoyed entertainment together, visited relatives together. When it came to family economics, we only bought what we could afford. The values represented by that family scene of long ago are: family stability; respect for authority; accountability for one's actions; working hard; and relationships taking precedence over individualism and independence.

Now how do we seniors help to restore the value system with which we were raised? The old fashioned way is the answer, and that is by example to the younger members of our families and, when the opportunity presents itself, to other young people outside the family. This can be done by getting involved in youth organizations like church youth groups, Boy Scouts and Girl Scouts, and sports activities.

Another way to influence the younger generation can and should come from the pulpits of our churches in a consistent and dramatic manner. Though some may try to separate religious values from governing, we have a long history of proving that government and society are better off when these values are held to steadfastly.

Self-denial as a Foundation

Self Denial – "Renunciation of your own interests in favor of the interests of others." It is my opinion we have lost the meaning of these words. They have been replaced with such phrases such as "Whatever," "What ever turns you on," Whatever makes you happy," "Go do your thing," "Who cares?" and I am sure there are more but they are not printable.

Self-denial helps us relate to another person with consideration. For example, self-denial was frequently practiced back in the days of the Depression. Individual self-denial was seen at the dinner table when there was not an abundance of food and families had to share. I learned that an empty stomach will give you a "wanting" feeling in your stomach as you lie on your "goose feather mattress" and try to go to sleep.

Self-denial was having thirty-five cents in your pocket and wanting to go to a movie but knowing you needed streetcar money the next day to go to school. Everything is relative and I am sure that you, my readers, can relate to these types of circumstances. It was tough when the guys on Saturday morning wanted you to play some ball but you had to go to your bakery job and earn some money instead.

There was the presence of self-denial when it came to obeying the laws of morality. But the society environment of the '30s, '40s, and '50s was one where it was expected that you would obey the laws of morality. I believe this expectation helped in practicing self-denial. Is self-denial practiced today? It is my opinion that it is rare. As I said in the beginning, we have become a society of "doing your own thing," which does not encompass the highest degree of self-denial, in my book.

Additionally, with everybody getting everything they want, as a rule, how much self-denial is required? Not much self-denial is required in a permissive society that accepts out-of-wedlock teen-age pregnancy, violence, profane language, morality, and divorce for frivolous reasons. The statistics show an alarming negative trend, which indicates to me there is not too much self-denial going on. In fact, we see just the opposite—self-gratification.

How about having a discipline when it comes to the management of your money? Instead of buying that car with all of the "bells and whistles," maybe you should buy the car that will give you excellent and dependable transportation. You can then take the difference in cost and put it into some type of savings to create a greater wealth. When you have the greater wealth in the bank, then you can do things such as buying that first home or saving for your retirement. There are many examples of self-denial that seniors could tell, but what it really boils down to is choosing between instant gratification now and a greater satisfaction in the long run.

When you are young, you are always faced with the decision of having what you want now or later. Short-term gratification or long-term satisfaction must be weighed to determine your course of action. As you get older, self-denial becomes more mandatory, such as in eating habits that can have an impact on your health or delaying a vacation because you have to put a new roof on the house.

To me, practicing self-denial helps to build strong character in an individual. This in turn prepares one for the times when he has to reach down within himself to find the strength to face the unpleasant things of life.

Self-denial can be in the simplest of forms. For instance, the doctor may tell you that you can have a cup of popcorn with no butter or salt. Show me the person who can do that and I want to shake his hand! By practicing self-denial in small ways, you will be better prepared for the big decisions that arise. Again, the young members of our families do recognize self-denial within the family unit and I believe they subconsciously respect that attribute of your character.

CHAPTER TWENTY-THREE

Attitudes That Count

Kindness

- Neighbors and Community

There was a time many decades ago when we were concerned about the trend of the economy downturn and worried about being able to buy a week's worth of groceries for twenty dollars. I can also remember when running a tab at the corner grocery store was commonplace for a lot of young married couples starting out. Some weeks I was unable to clear the whole tab, but our grocery man was a very warm-hearted and kind person to let this young family make sure we had food on the table. In fact, I remember that Mr. and Mrs. Steller were role models of kindness for this young couple. We were blessed to know them and be recipients of their kindness.

The kindness of our neighbors was also prevalent. When a member of the family was sick, the neighbors were there to help by bringing the proverbial chicken soup and a load of medical advice to us young inexperienced adults. An example of the kind of advice we received was, "Rub that Vicks Vaporub all over your chest, neck and back and then wrap yourself in a warm towel." The visits were not one-time happenings but continued until we were well.

Sometimes everyone in the community got involved in helping a neighbor. I remember when one of the outbuildings on my grandfather's farm was destroyed by fire. In no time, people from surrounding farms were there to help rebuild the building. A side benefit that I remember was that the ladies from an adjoining farm created those fabulous meals for the workers. Both the men's work and the women's cooking were spontaneous and were done in a spirit of true love from these people.

Another instance when I was shown kindness was in the upkeep of my first car. Since I did not know anything about cars, many of my neighbors helped out when my "jalopy" would be suffering from some type of problem. These problems encompassed anything from checking batteries to fixing mufflers. The method was to take a can and flatten it, wrap it around the hole in the muffler and then tie it on with a clothes hanger. Did it work? Yes, for a while, but then it was louder than if I had not tried the homemade remedy. However, I appreciated my neighbor's efforts, as I could not afford a new muffler.

In my early career trying to learn about punch cards (the pre-PC era), I was shown kindness by a first class petty officer known as Sam. He helped me in the evenings to learn what was to become my life's profession (now known as Information Technology). In turn, my wife and I would baby-sit for Sam and his wife when they wanted to have a night out, which usually meant seeing a movie on the base. We employed the barter system but to this day, some fifty-plus years later, I think of Sam and his extreme kindness shown to a seaman and his wife.

- *Kindness Shown by the Church Fellowship*

Today as mature citizens we are continually shown love and kindness by various prayer groups, as well as family members and friends. We all need some type of divine intercession to help us in our hour of need, but it appears that as we grow older, we personally have a need more frequently for this love and kindness. Having a church family gives more people the opportunity to show kindness when needed.

- *Random Acts of Kindness by Individuals*

Just think what a world this would be if we continually showed kindness to our fellow human beings. Kindness can be expressed in so many ways—by just having a smile on your face, by saying, "Good morning," by opening a door for someone or just saying, "Thank you, and you have a nice day," and really saying it from your heart.

Charity

Charity is defined as "A kindly and lenient attitude toward people." Have people become more charitable in our country than they once were? Today when we think of charity, we think of making a monetary donation that is tax deductible and good for the image of the donors, especially for celebrities and corporations. This was not true in the past. Regardless of motive, however, at least charitable funds are helping the unfortunate in our society. Sometimes it is just a need for temporary support to help them get back on track so that the recipients can become productive citizens again, depending on their individual circumstances.

In years past, charity seemed to be more from the heart. Two important elements in why this was true were the prevalence of family unity and an attitude of respect. There are many forms of charity besides giving money. I remember the old-time "hobo" that traveled by "riding the rails" (not in the paid passenger section, by the way). He would jump off of the freight train and take up temporary residence close to the train lines. Occasionally there would be a knock on the screen door on our back porch and there stood the man of the rails with his small carrying bag. He always had a beard but was dressed neatly and looked "scrubbed." "Is the lady of the house here?" was the question, or "Do you have any work that I can do in exchange for a meal?" The answer was always yes if in exchange he would do such chores as cutting firewood, clearing up a shed and other similar work—some kind of work effort to earn the meal. To me I saw this as an act of charity, because if he didn't do it, I was scheduled to have this on my "to do" work list.

Other acts of charity that came from the heart were numerous, such as bringing food to someone who was ill, doing farm chores for a farmer who was laid up, or cutting a neighbor's grass. The most memorable act of charity that happened each year was at harvest time when all of the farmers and their work hands would team up to bring in the harvest. The tremendous meals prepared by the ladies were for everyone to enjoy together after a hard day's work. One might say this was just a way to survive by joining together in order to bring the crops in on schedule—and one would be correct in saying that. However, if you had been there to see the love and charity that was so prevalent, you would know it was from the heart. I even knew that when I was still "wet behind the ears."

There were similar acts of charity from the heart in the big cities. I remember people's automatically shoveling snow off the sidewalk and driveway for the elderly, picking up the paper when it was raining really hard and taking the paper to the door so that the elderly did not have to weather the storm. These were common deeds done without being asked. I am not saying that charity today has no heart, but I would suggest that in the old days, charity was surely heartfelt!

Yes, we have acts of charity done today and by people who want to remain anonymous and those acts are from the heart. But it seems they are the exception rather than the rule. In my opinion, what we have today is not done freely or automatically but with some hidden agenda. I don't know but I am pretty sure the taxpayer of forty and fifty years ago did not get tax write-offs as a side benefit to offering charity.

What should we do? There is no pat answer, but I would suggest that when you are given the opportunity to provide a kindly act, search your heart and ask yourself if you would want to do this act for someone without any recognition or monetary gain. It is amazing the inner happiness you will receive when helping your fellow human being with pure motives.

Accountability

Accountability is simply being responsible for those things that you can control. I offer my opinion on this matter not from an academic viewpoint, as I am not qualified to do so, but from real life experiences that I know my fellow seniors have also had.

I love the meaning of this word as it is dynamic and impacts everything that we do in life. It impacts our social life, our workplace, our families and life in general. I believe one of the most important aspects of accountability is for us to realize that we are responsible for our words and actions and that we cannot blame someone else when things do not work out well. We must recognize and accept our responsibilities.

At an early age we are introduced to accountability. When we start school we become responsible to learn the basic subjects of reading, writing and arithmetic. As we go beyond this basic level, we continue to be responsible as we climb the educational ladder.

On the way, we also are learning we have other responsibilities, such as doing assigned chores or earning money to help pay for higher education. We learn that we are not here just to please ourselves, but others are counting on us as well. They care because they love us and are interested in seeing our progress in life.

Our next step in this process is entering the work force and, in some cases, choosing a lifetime partner and having children. Now the degree to which and number of things for which we become accountable has increased tremendously. What are these things for which we are accountable? The following are some of these responsibilities:

• Attitude in the Workplace

When your employer hires you to perform a job, you are accountable for the performance of task(s) for which in you will receive compensation. The assumption is that both parties have full understanding of the employment agreement—tasks to be performed and what the compensation for the work will be. It has been my firsthand experience that in the corporate world that people do not want to be held accountable for tasks that they were hired to do (I am sure it exists throughout the working environment and not just limited to the corporate world). Case in point: they sidestep their accountability in various ways such as: "This is not my task but someone else's" or "Let's form a committee to resolve this problem"

(Note: accountability has been shifted to a "no face person"—a committee). If something goes wrong, the committee can be blamed but if it goes right, everyone claims they were on the committee. Sound familiar? Enough on the work place, as this could be a book in itself.

- Accountability in the Family

Let's look at accountability as it relates to our families. Accountability as a member of a family unit can run the gamut from providing food and shelter to providing leadership relative to the social aspects of life. It also entails being a positive role model in the family and the community. In something as simple (note I didn't say "easy") as paying your debts, you are teaching accountability to your children and establishing your reputation in the community.

- Personal Benefits

Accountability, to me, is just another ingredient in making the complete person. If we accept the accountability for which we are responsible, we will benefit in ways that help us feel strong and competent, as well as complete as a person. At times it will be rough but we need to stand up and be accountable. Someday all of us will have to stand up before God and be accountable for the way we have lived our lives. We need to think about that now so we will be ready then.

Shame

Shame – "A painful emotion resulting from an awareness of inadequacy or guilt." In my opinion, our society has developed an acceptance of a "no shame" attitude towards living, as if we are accountable to no one, least of all God. Many years ago we avoided shame as if it were a dreaded disease. If we were reprimanded in school, it brought shame to the family and in turn the family heads would issue a reprimand that would fit "the crime." Right or wrong, there was no questioning by parents as to the authority of the school. In hindsight I can see that this was good and would be good to practice today because it shows a united approach by educators and parents to not only teach our children the subject matter, but to provide discipline in their everyday lives. I am sure there are many people today who would question the school's actions and, rather than work with the teacher very discreetly to resolve the issue, there is an attitude of "My child wouldn't do that" or "Don't you dare pick on my child!" I am not a teacher but I have an educator in my family and have friends who were educators and there is a fear that punishing a child for wrongdoing is not "politically correct." Think about that one for awhile and draw your own conclusions.

* * * * *

Historical Tidbit from 1960
Birth control pill developed and available for sale.

* * * * *

There is apparently no shame for immoral actions such as out of wedlock births and adultery. This is commonplace. Hollywood celebrities and public leaders have mistresses and children out of wedlock. These are people whom our children look up to and want to grow up to be like. In recent years, we have seen the devastation that can come as a result of this shamelessness. President Clinton, when confronted with his adulterous behavior, tried to sidestep the issue at hand by giving his definition of what a certain act was, with no sense of shame or responsibility. Apparently society accepted his definition, as there was no outcry of shame. In fact, millions of the American public went to the Internet for an account of the impeachment proceedings, where they could read all the sordid details of the testimony given in this case! From my perspective, having grown up in the '30s and '40s, this was not only a shameful but totally unacceptable act. I seem to remember that this definition was later used as a precedent in a court case in Texas. I assume that our society has no shame regarding this type of behavior and it is okay. No shame! No shame! I find it shameful that we are setting a precedent that will be acceptable to future generations. This is not only shameful, it is sad. In the good old days, public figures that acted in such immoral ways would have been removed from office. I remember a famous actress who was blacklisted after her immoral actions were leaked out to the public. This public exposure resulted in her being unemployed. Of course there were high public officials and other celebrities who were less than honorable in our day but their sins were "swept under the rug," and didn't became public knowledge at the time. Had it been known at the time, the historians might have written history a little differently.

To have shame (a sense of guilt) is good in that we recognize what is right from wrong. All of us have done things in our lives that we we're ashamed of and I am sure we will again in the future, not by design, but just because we are human beings. Having a sense of shame is a deterrent to doing those shameful acts in the future. It would be good for us as individuals and society as well if we had standards of morality that would help us clearly see when an action is sinful. It is only when we admit our sinfulness to God that He can forgive us and free us to be all that He created us to be. Until we do this as a society, we are lost.

Attitude toward Work

I want to compare the modern-day workplace environment with that of the late 1940s and 1950s. Keep in mind the things that have contributed to these changes. One of the factors that changed the working environment was the advent of the GI bill for the veterans, affording them a higher education, which otherwise may not have been attainable. Also, there was an increase in the need for trade schools, which was great, as the jobs were plentiful but trained employees were not. Houses were made available for many returning GI's due to the availability of VA loans in purchasing homes. This, as I remember, created a housing boom and, in turn, employment of veterans from the trade schools. Automobile mechanics were in demand and the automobile trade schools were there for individuals to get the training required for employment in the automobile industry. There was also available quite a diversity of jobs. This was a new working environment. Overtime pay was welcomed in order to pay for these newly acquired opportunities and assets.

In the late fifties we saw the beginning of the technology revolution. This to me has been one of the greatest factors that has not only changed the working environment but global economics, communications and business. We must recognize that information is considered essential for individuals, corporations and governments. Taking these two factors into consideration, we can see the evolution of a new workplace environment as compared to the forties, fifties and sixties, with even more change in the seventies and eighties.

- Appearance

It used to be expected if a man worked in an office, he wore a shirt and tie and, if in management, either a sport coat or suit. As a rule, our workday was 8:00 a.m.-5:00 p.m., with an hour lunch break. We normally brought our bag lunches and would eat in the lunchroom or on nice days we would go out and sit on the grass and enjoy lunch with our fellow workers. As I remember, those were very enjoyable times. We also had more small parks in which we could eat our lunch and take a walk because we didn't require all of the parking places that we need today. Most of us rode the streetcars and buses to work. Again, when we were asked to work overtime, it was like getting a blessing that would help us to support our families. Also in the '40s, '50s, '60s, there was only one working member of the family, which was one of the reasons why overtime dollars were greatly welcomed.

Now let's do some comparison as it relates to the office workplace environment. Today we have a predominance of companies allowing personnel to utilize a flextime work schedule. This means workers can vary their starting and quitting times with the sanction of the company.

Because of technology, some of the work force today can work from home. These workers include programmers, consultants, insurance and real estate agents, among others. Work attire today is usually casual dress. It started with Friday's being a day for casual dress, but it has been my experience that the dress code for the workplace is totally casual.

It has also been my experience that overtime is not necessarily welcomed by most employees. I don't know if it is just an aversion to work or if it is due to both spouses' working—maybe it is a combination of both.

- An Attitude of Loyalty

I am of the belief that loyalty to companies has vanished, for the most part. It is my opinion that companies have brought this on themselves when they started introducing words into the workplace such as: downsizing, re-engineering, bankruptcy, golden parachute, mergers and more mergers. In these mergers, it is like the big fish eating the little fish and then the bigger fish eating the next one. So today the environment of the workplace has become a "look out for me" attitude.

The days of receiving the gold watch at retirement seem to have vanished and the workplace does not look like it did some years ago. We seniors had a dedication to our companies that we do not see in the younger generation today. I believe that in the 80s, companies started thinking more about the "bottom line" than they did about their employees. With the corporate attitude (as exhibited in the Enron scandal, for example) we have lost respect for our employers, resulting in less loyalty to the job. The current work environment not only does not allow retirees to look forward to receiving that gold watch at the end of a long and faithful career, it is uncommon now to even work for the same company for most of your professional life.

- Ambition

I have seen a decline of ambition among the work force of today. Maybe it's a case of trying to hold onto the job they have and not wanting to rock the boat. Maybe employees have more outside interests, which results in less ambition for their jobs. Ambition is good as long as you always put your family first, and it is my opinion that this can be done. I feel that we must have ambition in order to succeed in our jobs, which should result in the ability to provide a comfortable life for our families. Ambition with integrity is great for self-esteem and, in turn, contributes to the greater good of society.

- Integrity

We seniors were not perfect in our younger working days, but I will say we had integrity. We come from a time when the mere shaking of hands was as good as a written contract. We believed in being people whose word was taken seriously and we knew that when we gave our word, it meant following through on the agreement.

Can we in this day and age that is so characterized by a fast-paced progression in technology and science still be people who couch their ambitions in integrity and loyalty?

I believe we can if we get back to the values that once were held by the majority of people in this country.

Drive Friendly

Back in the good old days, we did not have the traffic "crime" level that we have today. Everything is relative of course, for we did not have the traffic problems, the number and speed of the cars, the amount of travel, the transient work force or the super highways. We had gravel roads in the country and mostly paved two-lane interstate highways. Another thing that I remember is how the traffic laws were obeyed. "Stop" meant "stop"—no running stops allowed. Drivers took their turns at an intersection. This practice was common not only because it was the law but it was generally accepted as the courtesy of the road. To get a traffic ticket was an embarrassment. Today we are constantly in a hurry to get somewhere, resulting in a driving pattern that is hazardous. When you stop to think about it, how much time are you actually saving if you speed through a red light or do not come to a full stop at the stop sign? Hours? Minutes? How about seconds? I think, if we're truthful, those few seconds saved really do not justify our reckless driving habits. We have a new term today called "road rage." This has replaced what we did in the good old days. We called our outings with family, "going for a Sunday drive." That difference in terminology speaks volumes about the differences in mentality today as compared to days gone by. Society is spending scads of money on what causes road rage. Wow! I just can't understand what causes road rage—very interesting. I guess it will take a rocket scientist to figure that one out!

What we had, as a rule, was fear of the consequences of breaking the law and respect for life and the fear of doing bodily injury to ourselves as well as our fellow human beings. We also were able to focus on driving the car. We did not have other "tasks" to contend with as we have today. While driving, have you ever been guilty of:

- talking on the phone
- drinking a beverage
- shaving
- putting on make-up
- doing eye brows
- combing your hair
- reading something
- reading your palm computer
- changing clothes (yes, I said changing clothes)
- and finally, in some cases, having a "smoke?"

And we wonder why there are so many accidents and traffic violations! With all the other people on the road engaged in various distracting activities, I find it a full time job to just drive my car so I won't be hit by one of them!

As a young person it was an earned privilege to drive the family car. Today it appears that it is an automatic thing that the young person gets his own car when reaching driving age. My experience with earning this privilege was obtained by demonstrating maturity, accepting responsibilities, having acceptable school grades, and being accountable. The driving test given by the family member, friend or relative was a mental and physical challenge. In some ways, driving was more physically demanding, as we did not have automatic transmissions. No wonder we were advised to keep our eyes on the road and our hands on the wheel!

Today, at traffic lights, "red" for a lot of drivers does not mean stop but rather a signal to put your foot on the gas because of the rush to get someplace or, in some cases, a type of mental game to beat the light. It is not a rarity to see these violators having little children in the car. That is really scary, for what could be more important than the welfare of our little ones? How many times do you get ready to go on the green light when the person who has the red light accelerates, putting you in danger of being hit broadside? The blood rushes to your head, your hands become sweaty with the fear of what could have happened. Today I don't assume drivers will stop on red and before I accelerate, I assure myself that it is safe to proceed. I have learned to check for the "speeding bullet" that might just run a red light. This has become part of my driving standard.

Today, getting traffic violation tickets is a way of life. There doesn't seem to be any embarassment or second thoughts of what could have happened. In addition, it becomes a challenge to get a person to accept responsibility for his errors in driving. Try driving the speed limit and see how many drivers speed around you, at times endangering other motorists.

What can we do? I feel that when we are given the opportunity to educate new drivers, let us teach them about the do's and don'ts of driving such as: focus only on driving, practice road courtesy, obey the traffic laws, be patient and get rid of the stress before you get behind the wheel. Remember, a vehicle is a necessity in today's society and driving can be a pleasure but it can also kill or disable a person and impact the lives of their loved ones. Obey the traffic laws and have the proper awareness and attitude when you get behind the wheel. Sometimes the old advice is the best: "Keep your eye on the road and yours hands on the wheel."

Patience Makes Perfect

- Patience in Driving

According to the dictionary, impatience is defined as "a lack of patience; irritation with anything that causes delay." I guess nowhere is impatience shown in our society as it is on our super-highways. When I was young, I did not see obscene gestures, hollering at and threatening other drivers and people fighting on the highway. I believe that we did not have these problems because, as a whole, we were much more patient than drivers today. What do we have today? I see evidence of impatience everyday when driving. I guess I notice it more today as I am retired and I don't have that sense of "do or die" urgency. I do remember the day I converted from being an impatient driver to a patient one. I was driving home (on Highway 70) from my job that was located in downtown St. Louis after a stressful day of work. I was going in and out of my lane, trying to get ahead of everyone when it dawned on me what was I doing. I realized that this was making me a nervous wreck and, secondly, I was endangering my life and the lives of my wife and four children, as well as the lives of others on the road. In addition, when I got to a stop sign, invariably the car or cars that I was passing showed up at the same time at the same place. So I gained nothing in time or distance but I did get a lot of stress. All this because I was impatient. Being impatient will just add another load of stress, with no evident benefits. This will impact you in your work and in your relationships.

- Patience at Work

By and large I remember that in the past we were a nation of very patient people. We were patient because all of life moved at a slower pace. With the advancement in technology and the abundance of time-saving devices that have been invented, we seem to think it is our "right" to have everything done instantly. We experience this in our daily living with convenient appliances used at home, rapid mass transit and fast cars, and instant communications. All these things allow us to not only get places faster (giving us a fast forward mentality), but open up whole new worlds to us as we learn of events on the other side of the world even as they are happening.

Today, as never before, we have come to expect instant communication, whether it be at home or in business. Corporations have divisions throughout the world, necessitating instant communication for the purpose of making important decisions. We are a nation reliant on imports, as is noted by our current trade imbalance, and we need to know what is going on across the globe. We are able to communicate with them dynamically via the Internet. In business, we are able to have meetings with many attendees from various organizations via the teleconferencing capability. We are able to have technical work done in foreign lands and have that information immediately, unlike the old days when that work had to be done in the same building. So in the business world, you might say that our motto is, "We want it now!" We are very impatient.

Outside of the world of business, we now have friends and relatives not only located in other parts of the country but in foreign lands. With the advent of globalization, we now have opportunities to take vacations undreamed of back in the "good old days," when only the "rich and famous" had that privilege. I can just imagine someone from my place of birth taking a European vacation. We thought it was great just watching the new cars go through town!

But time marches on and now we do have these tremendous advancements in technology, sciences, transportation, communications, etc. However, with advancement comes this stressful condition called impatience.

- A Remedy for Impatience

I am sure that we all have various ways to handle impatience. I know that when I was employed there were times that I could "blow my stack," but I learned that does not accomplish anything but rather it only adds fuel to the fire in whatever situation in which I find myself. So what I learned to do was to take a walk and talk to myself—I don't recommend you do it out loud or others may wonder about you—and take some deep breaths. You know what? It works. Here's another recommendation for stress relief. If you can afford it financially and can take some time off, I recommend that you stay at a hotel right on the ocean and let the waves lull you to sleep at night and awaken you in the dawn's light. Wow, what therapy! As the saying goes in Hawaii, "Hang loose." Patience is a by-product when you take this approach to stressful situations.

The Blame Game

Did you ever notice that when anything goes wrong in our country, immediately the blame game starts? It is my opinion it is politically driven to get some one-upmanship against political rivals. In August 2003, the New York grid electrical system went down and millions of people were without power. The residents of many cities were caught as they were leaving work. It did not take long for the blame game to start, as that very evening the senator from New York was on the radio blaming the President's administration. Yet no one knew at that point what the cause was, so how could anybody blame someone when the cause was not even known? As for this blackout, there was no one political party to blame, as they had nothing to do with it. This includes the legislative and the executive branches of government. The following Sunday, it seemed all the "talking heads" on television were giving their take on the situation. I just wanted to shout, "Why don't you all keep your mouths shut until you find out what the problem is?" It would have been good to report the problem and offer possible remedies, instead of trying to place blame. In situations like this, there should be a plan in place and a determination by the major responsible parties to implement such a plan. Reports should be made to the nation stating the progress on each major non-sensitive milestone of a problem-solving plan. Furthermore, someone must be held accountable for this plan—not a committee or group but one person. If the plan does not progress, we should get a replacement to do the problem solving, unless there is "just cause" that the plan failed. Wouldn't it be great if we the citizens would be informed without wasting time on the blame game? That's what we do in the private sector and it works. I guess the reason it works is that we have to resolve problems in a timely, quality and cost-effective manner. The Washington "inner circle" ought to try it—it is really rewarding.

* * * * *

Historical Tidbit from 1965
10 November – The biggest power cut in history
hit some northeastern states and parts of eastern Canada.
About 30 million people found themselves in the dark.

* * * * *

The blame game has to stop, as it is very childish. If you "foul up," say so and state what you are going to do about it. Wouldn't that be refreshing? Depending on the severity of the foul-up, the individual may be given the chance to take action and solve the problem. That person would be respected for his integrity.

We are living in a different world today than we were thirty, forty or fifty years ago. There are many nations that are envious of our freedoms and this has been made obvious by the United Nations' actions. There are terrorist cells in many foreign nations. It is my opinion as a common citizen that we are so vulnerable because we are a free and open society. Our borders are open on both sides. We have many ports with millions of tons of goods arriving from other countries. We have the open skies. We have energy plants, dams, bridges, railways, transportation, financial centers, and the list goes on and on. This is not to alarm anyone but, from my perspective, this places us in a very vulnerable position. This is another area in which we the public should require a "report card" relative to the planned objectives of assuring security at the state and federal levels. Now maybe I missed it, but I hear the news every morning and evening and I am not alone in being very interested in the progress of our security efforts. Now it is a given that we the citizens do not need to know all the details about what's being done if broadcasting this knowledge would jeopardize our security. But, based on the past track records of some, we are skeptical about the effectiveness of security measures. We need to be reassured by our nation's leaders that the job of security is getting done and that we as citizens of this nation can count on the most complete and best protection that can be given. It is my view that we will never have perfect security, as we are an open society, but our leaders must do the best they can without playing the "blame game." I believe they should work together as a team, regardless of political agendas and personal egos. This is what we elect them to do. They are to be working for us, not just stoking the fires of their own political aspirations. Our elected and appointed officials must constantly be reminded that even though some of us did not wear shoes when we were growing up and we may be considered naïve about worldly matters, God and our Constitution has given us the right to be informed of matters that affect us all.

None of us lives in a cave and we know what is happening out there in the world relative to tragedies such as 9/11, the Northeast blackout and terrorist activity. Most of all, let us not put ourselves in the position of just being reactive to tragedies but rather let us be proactive relative to those things that we can control. We have some of the smartest and most dedicated people living in this country that are responsible for our well being. So, why shouldn't we expect them to act as good stewards of the trust given them by our nation's citizens? This would be the course of wisdom.

Wisdom of the Ages

Wisdom is more than an attitude, although that is one characteristic of it. Wisdom is applying the knowledge you have in a reasonable and wise way. This wisdom usually comes from personal experience. However, the younger generation does not always appreciate it when you are giving advice. Isn't it amazing that when your children get older, they wonder how you got so smart? They don't realize that we the parents have always had intelligence through each stage of their lives.

By the time we become grandparents, we have already experienced many things in life by becoming a parent, raising children, interfacing with the schools, and managing an income to support a family and all their needs.

We have learned through trial and error and have added to our reservoir of knowledge, giving us the ability to advise others. But it appears to me that society as a whole does not utilize the wisdom that comes from our cumulative life experiences. This is not "Artificial Intelligence" (for the reader well-versed in technology) but it is real, live, and comes with an authenticity that is far from being artificial.

There are some companies, especially large corporations that employ a Board of Directors, that rely on the expertise of those who have much experience. With their experience and knowledge they can help guide the development of business strategies that will result in success. Now these boards usually are made up of people who are still active in the work force and some who are retired from successful careers. Now this being the case, why can't seniors be used in an advisory capacity in all facets of the work environment?

Here is a possibility: using seniors as consumer advisors for grocery stores and other retail stores, helping to develop marketing strategies. Now one might think this suggestion has no validity. Well! At the age of seventy and gainfully employed by a very prestigious technology corporation, I was frequently flown into the home office to review marketing strategies for a new technology product from the viewpoint of a consumer who would be buying the new product. Why me? Well, in a prior position with a different company, I was responsible for the purchasing of technology products. So who better than I, even at seventy years of age, to ask the piercing questions like: "Would there be a market for the product?" "Who would be the target customer?" and "What should the marketing plan look like?" This is but one example of what a senior can offer to the business world. Another advantage of using me was that I was already retired from another company so I could speak freely, as I was not trying to climb the corporate ladder, hence not being a threat to the young up-and-comers.

In the most recent war in Iraq, did you notice that all the major networks had retired military officers doing an analysis of the strategies of the war? This is again an example of how seniors still have a role to play in life if they so desire. In addition, people who formerly had roles in resolving world issues are quite frequently brought back into government service to resolve issues, due to their life-long wisdom.

When I was employed at a major corporation, a gentleman was about to retire. This was going to cause a major problem, as he was the only one in this company that had the knowledge to carry on the major tasks of buying futures. My department was called on to solve this problem by utilizing a technology system called Artificial Intelligence. Generally speaking, this was to capture all of his case scenarios and decision processes and then convert the decision routines into a computer program. After this gentleman retired he was called on from time to time to fine-tune the system. The point is, with the use of technology, we captured this senior's decision-making process, so in essence the senior lives on. Remember that the only way the system was born in the first place was due to the life-long experiences of this individual. It was wisdom on the part of the company to access the cumulative wisdom of this very experienced worker.

While growing up in the '30s and '40s, I remember that senior citizens (although they weren't called that then) were often consulted in various situations, and their words were respected. It seems that today that we seniors are not consulted that frequently about certain issues. I feel that we seniors have a lifetime of experiences on varied subject matters, ranging from social to business issues. I know that from time to time I am consulted on issues and there are other times when I interject my thoughts for consideration.

Wisdom is gained through the trials and tribulations of life and it would be a shame for the younger citizens of this nation not to take advantage of this hard-earned knowledge when the opportunity presents itself, whether it be in the business or social arena of life.

What Makes You Happy? What Makes You Sad?

The following are my thoughts from a senior's perspective as to what makes people happy and what makes them so sad. Now I know that all of you might not agree with me because what might make me happy might make you sad and the reverse is also true. For example, when the St. Louis Cardinals baseball team beats their rival the Chicago Cubs, I am elated but you, loving the Chicago Cubs, will be sad. At the same time, we can both be happy in that we love the game of baseball. The most important thing for us as seniors is to stay alert and recognize happiness in whatever form it takes, for it is all too easy to recognize sadness and dwell there.

Happiness, joy, gladness, satisfaction or pleasure can be summed up in this definition (Vandegriffe version): feeling good, with sunshine in your heart. In the dictionary, sadness is defined as: "emotions experienced when not in a state of well-being." Sadness for me is when I am downhearted and I have the strong desire to fight those things that have made me sad.

Now having set the stage, I want to discuss some specifics of what affects my moods—not only mine but many seniors' with whom I have talked. I am very happy when my entire family gets together to have a meal and enjoy one another's company. They start telling stories on each other about when they were growing up, thinking that Mom and Dad did not know about their activities.

Maybe they thought we did not know about some of those happenings, but we did and were just silent at the time. But the happy part is when they start exaggerating on a given story—followed by laughter by the entire family. It's an unofficial game of who can tell the most ridiculous story now in front of their parents. What happiness! My wife and I continue to get joy as we repeat these stories later when it's just the two of us.

What makes me sad is when I know of lonely people. Now maybe they are truly happy by being alone—I don't really know. Of course being alone doesn't always mean one is lonely. Based on my observation and conversation, however, my interpretation is that many are lonely. I try the best I can to make some of that loneliness leave by talking about what's happening in their lives now and have them share some of their pasts as well. I try to encourage them to talk about when they were in the work force, playing a sport, participating in activities at school or their political opinions. That gets them going. So maybe if we think that someone is lonely, we can very discreetly try to eliminate some of that loneliness. The forum for these discussions can be luncheons or just phone calls.

What else makes me happy besides family gatherings? Some of the first signs of spring such as: the first sighting of buds appearing on the trees; the baseball pitchers and catchers reporting to spring training; constantly watching the flowers coming up through the ground; seeing the birds in flight with the material in their beaks for their nests in preparation for their new families. There are so many more signs and happenings that make spring such a happy time of the year.

Now just the opposite makes me sad: signs of winter approaching. I find that the older I get, the more I dread those cold and dreary days. When we are young, we enjoy all the seasons. I remember some twenty years ago when we had a period of some three weeks in which we did not see the sun. At that same time, the corporation that I worked for had a large meeting in which the chief executive officers dealt with how the corporate family was feeling depressed due to not seeing the sun for so many weeks. We termed it the "gray sickness." Naturally, we all needed some motivational pep talks to help us get through that period. I thought that this was a very appropriate measure taken by the management.

What made us happy or sad as we were growing up in the '30s and '40s? For us who grew up in the small towns or on farms, happiness came in the simple things, like when at Christmas time we would go to church and they gave all of the kids a big brown bag filled with candy, fruit, and nuts. How about getting some new boots or corduroy pants? I remember the little girls getting home-made dolls, most of which looked like Raggedy Ann's. One of the most popular gifts for the adults was the homemade quilt. None of these were all terribly expensive and they were gifts of the heart. Boy, how the times have changed! The expectation for Christmas gifts is very different today.

I remember sad times too. What made me sad was when: a farmer's crop did not come in due to the lack of rain; when a man got hurt in a wood mill or injured while fixing some farm equip-ment; when an unshaven man in dirty clothes knocked at the door to ask if he could do some chores in exchange for food. And I remem-ber so vividly how I felt as he washed up with water and soap by the cistern. I felt that he was so lonely.

What made all of us sad was when the men headed off to war. Dads, uncles, brothers, friends were reporting to the draft boards and in matter of weeks were leaving for the service, having no idea what was ahead of them and fearful of who was going to fill the void at home, providing food for the table and bringing in the crops. Some men were in their late thirties, but due to their job skills, were being drafted. Anxiety and sadness were prominent words that can be used to describe that period of time in our history.

On the flip side was when the men and women came marching home. VJ Day (the date of Allied victory over Japan, World War II) was a sight to behold. Everyone was happy that the war was over. As mentioned in an earlier chapter, another happy time was when the veterans could buy a home or start or continue receiving higher education due to the passage of the GI Bill.

The seniors of today can be happy that we grew up and experi-enced an era of respect, morality, little crime, clean entertainment for the whole family, and many other blessings. It is my opinion that we seniors should remind the younger generation of those values with which we grew up whenever the opportunity presents itself.

We have and will continue to have periods of sadness and happiness in our lives but that is life as we know it here on earth. Let's remember to enjoy and savor the things that make us happy. Let's not dwell on the sad times because we may just miss that next opportunity to be happy. Let us remember also that for those of us who have a relationship with God that we can look forward to the time in the life to come when we will know the fullness of joy without sadness, pain, or tears. That, my friends, will be true happiness without end.

Choose Your Destiny

We are truly blessed in that we live in a country in which we can choose our own destinies. When I talk about destiny, I mean all aspects of living—such as our choices and courses of action regarding profession, faith, morality, social behavior—and our approach and attitude towards life as a whole. We need to ask, "What is my purpose in life?"

When I was growing up, it was in an era of "high standards" regarding all aspects of being a human being and a citizen of the community. So to me this environment kept me on a stricter path, giving me boundaries in which to determine my destiny. Contrast this with the attitude of the younger generation of the late '60s, who wanted no boundaries. I believe this attitude has led to our current problems with violence, crime, addictive behavior, high divorce rate and a permissive society.

* * * * *

Historical Moment from 1969
The hippies' counterculture of peace and love, born in San Francisco four years ago, is sweeping across the US and Europe. The Woodstock Festival in New York (November 1969) drew 400,000 young people who camped out and shared drugs for three days as they listened to anti-war bands and singers.

* * * * *

After World War II and the birth of the "baby boomers," the next great employment explosion was in the technology field. Today technology is the lifeline for our citizens and corporations in their everyday living. From a professional point of view, we have so many opportunities to choose our destiny.

* * * * *

Historical Tidbit from 1980
The Japanese electronic firm *Sony* is not marketing its "Walkman," a new portable, shockproof, stereophonic radio-cassette player.

* * * * *

When it comes to choosing your destiny (which could be defined as your "fate"), I see that today our citizens have a real challenge they must face—especially younger people. The young are faced with questions like, "What is my attitude towards a career? Do I want to do all the things required to enter my chosen career? Do I want to make the sacrifice, if required? Am I willing to start at the bottom of the ladder, and to take the time to advance? Do I want to advance?" The answers to these questions will help to determine their professional careers. It is exciting for me to see many young people pursuing the opportunities presented to them, giving them fulfilling careers and helping them to be contributing members of society.

Now in pursuing career goals, I hope that these young people will realize that they need to make family a priority. This is just foundational for a successful, functioning society.

It is my opinion that this is a real challenge today because we are living in a very self-centered, permissive society. In my day, it was a given to say prayers at public functions, to have the Ten Commandments displayed, and have nativity scenes displayed at Christmas time in front of City Hall. Marriage was considered sacred and permanent. Many long-held traditions were honored and I believe that gave us a more stable culture. That is why I said earlier that my destiny decisions were guided by well-defined standards and I am glad they were there.

We are so fortunate that we have the opportunity to determine our own destiny, as far as career path, marriage and family are concerned. Beyond these choices, it is even more important to determine our purpose—what we are here on earth for—and for that, we must look to our Creator God.

* * * * *

Historical Moment from 1962
John Glenn is the first American to orbit the Earth.

* * * * *

Waking Up to Reality

As we seniors continue to grow older and older, there are moments when we realize we need to wake up to what is important in our lives. Our lives should not be defined by our wealth or material goods, but rather by the love we share with our families, friends and those we meet each day. Relating to others can be something as simple as a smile or expression of thanks.

You know the saying that goes "you can't take it with you." This saying is true. Every rich and famous person finds out in the end that they are just normal people like you and me and that their fame and fortune cannot deter the ultimate.

Here is a short story to illustrate life's time span. My wife and I bought a new home several years ago and my daughter bought a tree for the yard as a present. She told us to go to the nursery and see if we liked what she had picked out for us. Well, we arrived at the nursery and they showed us this rather small tree. We asked how fast did this tree grow and the man told us its growth was a few inches a year. Well, this wouldn't do, so he showed us several other trees and the story was the same. I stated that we would not be able stay around on this earth to enjoy the full growth. So we used our daughter's gift towards a tree that was eighteen feet tall. She fully understood.

We need to focus on the important things in life. That means not worrying about the future. For instance, I am not going to worry about the interest rates, the value of the dollar, or what political party will be in power in 2012. Now this may sound like I'm giving up on life but that is not the case. At this stage of life I've already had decades of worrying about making a living, raising a family, getting the promotion, paying off the mortgage, etc. Now I am at a more relaxed time of life and I stop and smell the flowers, watch the trees begin to bud in the spring, visit our friends, be with our family, and take trips and vacations whenever possible.

As we realize what is important and take action to insure we enjoy life's blessings, we can do one additional thing. We can influence the younger generations in our families and help them realize what is important in life as well. Because of our cumulative experience and wisdom from lessons learned, we can help them to start appreciating the important things too. Let us share the happiness.

Perspective

Just think about how our roles have changed throughout our lives. As children we sat in the back seat of the car and for some of us we had to sit in a rumble seat in the back of a Model "A" or "T" Ford. We enjoyed the ride, while at the same time asking the universal questions, "When are we going to get there?" "When are we going to eat?" "I have to go to the bathroom," and "How long are we going to stay?" Now as adults we have taken on the role of responsibility for driving the car. We take this role seriously and we hold to the rules of driving safely by obeying the laws to assure passengers and pedestrians are kept out of harm's way. And for the parents who now have children sitting in the back seat, they are answering the questions that we once asked. How the roles have changed! Remembering our own childhood and young parenthood should help us to be patient with those who are asking the questions today.

In the area of education, our roles as children were to take responsibility to learn for ourselves the building blocks of knowledge that would help us not only to earn a diploma but also to prepare us for adulthood. This role prepared us to be a part of not only the work force but also society at large. The role of parents is to encourage their children to take advantage of these educational opportunities and to give their best efforts in the process.

In growing up, we as children take for granted that our physical, educational, emotional, and spiritual needs will be met by our parents or guardians. We also expect support from them in our life pursuits. Many young people expect their parents to pay their tuition and provide transportation for them as well. In this day and age I would venture to say that this is approaching the norm. I'm afraid it is also true for many that they have not been taught the value of a dollar and there is a rude awakening when they go out on their own and have to provide for themselves. Then as parents of adult children, our roles change again. We are now not "recipients" but "givers." This is essential, but also it is important that we are role models of integrity and that we provide direction for the young.

Now the roles have changed again. We find we are taking on the role of "patriarch" of the family—a position that has been earned throughout a lifetime as we accepted the roles that life presented to us. Now one might think that this role of patriarch is not important, but I beg to differ, because as the patriarchs, we continue to be positive role models. When asked, we provide alternative solutions to problems presented to us by members of the family but are careful to recognize the responsibility of the decisions lay upon the one that makes the request. We also inherit the honor of sitting at the head of the table for meals at family get-togethers. We now sometimes get to ride in the back seat of the car. It seems we have come full circle, does it not? We also get to sit in the most comfortable chair at Christmas time when presents are being opened. We are really on the sidelines of everyday problems that occur in life but we still are there to give our love, support and advice when called upon. We can wear the badge of patriarch proudly, as we have earned it.

No matter the stage of life in which we find ourselves, it is beneficial to evaluate our attitudes. In this chapter we have explored different areas in which attitude is important. I am sure that my readers can come up with more, and I hope you do. We need to think about how our attitudes not only benefit us but how they impact on others as well. We can to be agents of change for the good in our nation, so let us be good role models by having good, positive, uplifting, encouraging attitudes. This will take us far.

1980-1989
"A World of Contrasts"

The 1980s decade was a world of contrasts. The 80s saw the collapse of the Iron Curtain and the end of the Cold War. By the end of the decade, the signs were obvious that the Soviet Empire was in collapse. However, while European communism was dissolving and people in the West were becoming richer, drought, famine, and civil wars intensified in the Third World. Environmental issues aroused global anxiety, which led to a greater awareness in the US of damage to our earth and counteractive measures that could be taken.

International crises like the Iranian hostage situation in 1981, the war in the Falklands in 1982, the rise of AIDS epidemics, the nuclear disaster at Chernobyl in 1986, the Tiananmen Square massacre in Beijing and the fall of the Berlin Wall in 1989, began to shape the American presidency and increase the US role in "policing" the world.

In spite of the problems plaguing the nation, with the Reagan presidency came an air of "Don't Worry, Be Happy." The world shared the happiness of Prince Charles and Diana of England in their spectacular televised wedding. The first American woman to take a "ride" in space boarded the space shuttle *Challenger*, launching a new trend. Her name was Sally Ride. The movies had us looking beyond this earth for otherworldly fantasies and Rock stars climbed on the "Band-Aid" wagon, raising the consciousness of a nation to help the world's needy. The increased awareness of world hunger also was evident in the churches across our land as church groups and other organizations saw to the needs of the hungry. Computer technology continued to make great strides, which would influence many generations to come. The high-tech world of business and the low-income jobless—these symbolize the 80s as a "world of contrasts."

SECTION 6

SENIORS – ALIVE AND WELL

CHAPTER TWENTY-FOUR

A Profile of Today's Senior Citizen

W hat does today's senior citizen look like? For the most part, I have observed that seniors are respectful, courteous, upstanding citizens. Seniors are the prominent group at sporting events, where men take off their hats and hold them over their hearts and the ladies place their hands over their hearts while singing the National Anthem with pride in their voices. They also know the words and the enthusiasm shown while singing indicates they believe in the words.

When walking down the sidewalk, the man will make sure the lady is on the inside for her protection. While walking along the street or wherever, the man will nod or tip his hat as an act of courtesy to a lady. On entering a building, he will open the door to let a lady enter first. When entering an automobile, he will open the door while the lady gets into the car and, when they arrive at their destination, he will exit and open the door for the lady to exit from the car. He will let the lady off at the door if it is raining or if he has to park at some distance away. If a senior bumps into someone, he will apologize rather than saying, "Watch it!"

The seniors of today learned many courtesies while riding the bus or streetcar in days gone by. If there were no seats available and a lady got on board, a gentleman immediately gave up his seat for the lady. If a lady had too many packages, the gentlemen would help by holding some of them. While they were departing from the transport, the gentleman would help the lady off. The driver would patiently wait, which was also an act of courtesy

Seniors are embarrassed if someone curses in front of them or in front of children. While dining at a restaurant with friends or loved ones, they are embarrassed if at nearby tables there are loud conversations going on that contain embarrassing subject matter. The senior will politely remind them to hold their conversation down in order not to embarrass the people at his table.

Seniors are very trusting, coming from an era of not locking the doors, taking a person's word as sacred, doing business with a handshake, not locking the windows, leaving the keys in the car. It is a shock for them to live in the current environment. There is also no longer any respect of age when it comes to criminal acts. We have to legislate laws to protect us, whereas there was a time when crimes against the elderly would have been unthinkable.

It is the seniors who remember the Great Depression, World War II, Pearl Harbor, Guadalcanal, Normandy, and Hitler's Germany. They remember the beginning of the Atomic Age, the Korean War, the Cold War, the Jet Age, the moon landing, the first flight faster than sound and the Vietnam War. Throughout these decades, we learned our work ethics, the value of a dime, gratefulness, the need to save, the need to learn and get an education. Prior to World War II, the average person did not have these opportunities. We learned all these things and, in addition, we learned the true meaning of God, family, and country.

The vocabulary of a senior is typified by a lot of:

- "Yes m'am" and "No sir."
- "Thank you."
- "Excuse me."
- "I am sorry."
- "May I help you?"
- "May I get that for you?"

You may also notice they use the English language as the basis of communication. In contrast, there are words used today that I don't know if they are terms of endearment or vulgarity. Maybe it's just as well I don't know!

Finally, did you ever notice when dining out at a restaurant, going to a play or musical, going to church or other public gatherings how the seniors are dressed up? The gentlemen are wearing ties with sport coats or a suit and the ladies wear such fine dresses and their hair and nails are beautifully done—in other words, as we used to say "all fancied up." Well! I am proud to call myself a senior, as I wouldn't have it any other way.

Staying Young

Staying young is a state of mind, in my opinion. Come back with me as I to digress to the time when I was a young man and my attitude toward our mature citizens. The work ethics of the '30s, '40s, and '50s was that everybody worked. This being the case, our mature citizens continued working until they were unable to answer the "start bell." Let me define working as it is related to the mature citizen of that era. Some continued to do the same job that they had done in their younger years. It may not have been at the same speed, quantity or other degrees of measurement of what constituted productivity. Others would stay active in lesser jobs and not be required to work full time.

Senior citizens enjoyed their fishing, hunting, fixing their cars and other equipment and were great storytellers. They were also great weather forecasters, basing their forecasts on the appearance of the moss on trees, the sky, fur on the animals and other signs of nature. They were good and farmers relied on this analysis to determine what actions they would take as it related to their crops. The mature ladies became the cooking experts on how to can fruits and vegetables and participate in the church pie contests. I remember some of the quilts and other knitting and sewing pieces they created and sold to support a community cause. They would gather in each other's homes and "knit and purl" while they had conversations along with lemonade and "homemade cookies." By all appearances they were happy and contented—not bored. They generally had a good sense of humor, were up on current events, and were active participants in life.

I think it was a good idea for people to keep working as long as their health allowed. As a mature citizen myself, I find that my continuation in the workplace is very rewarding. I am with young people and stay attuned to "What's happenin'?"—not only in the workplace but life in general. I am able to contribute out of my life and work experience and I am freer to express my opinions in a professional manner because I'm not dependent on the paycheck to make a living. When I was young and raising a family, I was dependent on that paycheck, and this made me more timid.

Although I contribute to the work world, I still have time to pursue recreational activities. I am very active in playing racquetball. This is part of my health program and is a game that I totally enjoy and love the people with whom I compete. With my job and my entertainment activities filling my time, I do not have time to think about "What if?" situations or "Gosh, I am turning "X" number of years old on my next birthday."

I see so many mature citizens today who are using this approach to staying young. I saw a smiling, silver-haired gentleman the other day who was wearing a neatly pressed uniform. He was a maintenance man in this particular building and he was running up the stairs when I saw him. I saw him in the hallway busily working. I couldn't help myself but to go up to him and comment on his apparent happiness and work energy. I told him it was great to see another "gray-haired guy" hanging in there. I asked him if he would mind telling me his age. He said, "No problem," and that he was in his mid 70s and was happy and enjoying in what he was doing. We shook hands and, without a lengthy conversation, we both understood that we had a common approach to staying young.

There are so many opportunities to continue to participate in life—to be a volunteer for some worthy effort; to continue in your chosen profession at a lesser pace; or perhaps to change careers and doing something that you always wanted to do. This can be a time in your life to experiment and have fun, resulting in happiness—a refreshed and newfound happiness. In this pursuit you set the stage for communication with newfound friends and the ability to have discussions relative to the tasks at hand. Remember, age is a state of mind, so think forever young.

It's All in the Head

Sometimes we seniors, as we get older, get a little "cranky," so we must be cognizant of that. In addition we must realize that we are watching a new generation grow up and things are different than when we were growing up. The one exception to this is that we must continue fight to retain those moral values that were so prominent in the '30s, '40s and early '50s. This will always be a work in progress.

One area in which we practice having a good attitude is in driving. Driving just seems to take more concentration as we get older. There are classes for seniors to refresh their driving skills and, more importantly, to remind us of the courtesies and rules of the roads. We are never too old to learn. I certainly include myself in this category. As far as keeping a positive attitude towards driving is concerned, we need to keep our anger in check when we have to tolerate other people's driving habits. In a previous chapter, I have already discussed at length the modern-day perils of driving a car, so let that suffice.

I'll just share this funny story with you. I think you will get the point.

Two elderly women were out driving in a large car—both could barely see over the dashboard. As they were cruising along, they came to an intersection. The stoplight was red, but they just went on through. The woman in the passenger seat thought to herself, "*I must be losing it. I could have sworn we just went through a red light.*"

After a few more minutes, they came to another intersection and the light was red again. Again, they went right through. The woman in the passenger seat was almost sure that the light had been red but was really concerned that she was losing it. She was getting nervous.

At the next intersection, sure enough, the light was red and they went on through. So, she turned to the other woman and said, "Mildred, did you know that we just ran through three red lights in a row? You could have killed us both!" Mildred turned to her and said, "Oh my! Am I driving?" (Unknown Source)

CHAPTER TWENTY-FIVE

Activities for Seniors

Retirement – "The state of being retired from one's business or occupation." Well! I don't know if I am the one that should be writing about retirement but I will, because according to the unofficial rules of society, I guess I should be "hanging it up." Hanging it up suggests that when you retire, you just sit around and do nothing. However, even if you retire, there are still many ways to remain active, giving you a sense of satisfaction and usefulness. There are people who just simply stop working at their profession—but they still travel, play golf, or do craft work—and totally enjoy this type of retirement.

As a young man I really did not know many people who were retired. They may have retired from the job they had had for thirty to forty years and got their retirement watch, but they immediately went into some other type of employment, health permitting. I remember my grandfather who was a blacksmith and retired, as he could not stand up to the physical requirements that this job required. At age 60, he got involved in another means of employment. Most of the people I knew did physical labor and when they got close to their 70th birthdays, they automatically did something else—if nothing more then planting a vegetable garden and selling vegetables and fruit to the townspeople and the grocery stores. The town banker, the barber, and the county physician never retired. Now I am not saying this is good or bad but that is the way it was. So with that as my background, you can see the reason for my approach to retirement—I still work even though I have retired many times.

Retirement to me is the ability to do whatever you want to do whenever you want to do it. Naturally, this is dependent on your health, finances and consensus with your spouse if you are married.

For example, I know a retired professional person who now does craft work and does it well. I admire his talent. He has a workshop in his home and is so content in creating beautiful things. He sells these hand-crafted products but making money is not his objective. His objective is to be able to create beautiful objects that people admire. What a retirement and what a blessing!

I know of several persons who have retired from major firms and were once part of their management team and now they have gone back into the work force, doing jobs they did twenty years ago. Why? They like what they do and I must say they do an excellent job. I remember that during the Y2K emergency (computers and the problems connected with the new millennium) many of the retired folks were brought back into the work force, as these men and women had the expertise to solve the problem. And yes, there was a problem, believe me! The point is that seniors have much to offer even after the official retirement age.

* * * * *

Historical Tidbit from 1993
More and more people are "on the net,"
a computer network that links other networks,
and has the potential to reach anyone in the world.

* * * * *

Managing Your Time

Before we retired we had to manage our time in raising a family and working. For some of us, we also added night school, becoming students again and doing the homework. Then we were involved with the children's activities—everything from baseball games to dance recitals. So in order to accomplish these required tasks, we employed time management, something for which I attended seminars when I was working.

I am not saying that now that we are retired we have to have stringent rules on when, where and how we are going to do things. However, I want to challenge you to think about how time management can allow you to get more things done in a more enjoyable manner. Being actively engaged in life and doing so in a organized way will keep you young and bring a sense of accomplishment as well as enjoyment.

To employ time management, you must have a plan with which you are comfortable. I will bet that you do this today but you may not call it time management. You get up in the morning and discuss with your mate what you are going to do today. The conversation goes something like this: "What do you want to do today?" The reply is, "I don't know, what do you want to do today?" This dialogue goes on for some period of time. Wouldn't it be better to sit down on Sunday evening and write down a very simple plan concerning your activities for the week? There are certain things that are a constant, such as going to the grocery store, going to the hairdresser and so forth. So when you finish with the activities that are a must, maybe you have some days that are free. So maybe you can call a friend on Monday morning and schedule a luncheon or other get-together. Or perhaps you want to plan a day trip in the car to enjoy the countryside and buy some produce from a farmer's stand. Now if you have enough time, you may want to plan an overnight trip to see someone that is not so close to home.

This planning is dynamic. The plan makes you think of what, how and when you want to do some sort of task. As the week goes on, the plan may change due to unforeseen circumstances, but your plan can be adaptable. It is easy to modify your plan.

I personally plan twelve months out. The plan shows when we will be going on vacation, have scheduled dentist appointments or other doctor's visits, or meetings with the financial planner, tax man, or work activities I am aware of at the time of planning. Now when someone calls me for lunch, either for business or pleasure, I immediately know my availability. In addition, I immediately know when there is available time to take those day trips, call a friend for lunch and those other retiree free times.

Again, I know we retirees are "not on a schedule" but I find that by this time management planning I don't have to carry everything in my head, which is a little dangerous as we get older. We do have to contend with those senior moments. I know that I accomplish a lot more by doing this time management—a carry-over from when I was employed. I just wanted to share with you an idea for your consideration. If you are a person that is very involved in life and wants to do everything that you enjoy in your retirement—make a plan that fits your "retiree activity list." This will help eliminate some stress and confusion, resulting in everything that you do being more enjoyable.

Volunteering Your Time

Just recently I visited a relative in a hospital and, besides finding out that she was going to be okay, I saw something that really impressed me. It was a senior couple doing volunteer work in the hospital. Most of us are aware of these kinds of volunteers, but only at the subconscious level. So, in this section, I want to awaken our thoughts on the great work those seniors who volunteer their time, skills and compassion.

It is my opinion that the seniors perform the majority of volunteer work, being involved in hospitals, charity organizations, homeland security, youth organizations…the opportunities are endless.

It has been my experience that the rewards of volunteering are many. A volunteer, as defined by the dictionary, is: "A person who freely enlists for service." In giving freely of their time, volunteers do not expect monetary compensation or ego boosting but instead have an inward satisfaction that comes from having helped someone.

Volunteering may be in the form of sharing with a group of people who may have the same health condition that you have. You can discuss your own personal experiences and how you successfully manage your health condition. When it comes to health issues, we want to hear from the professionals, but I believe that we also like to hear from someone who is in the same condition that we are experiencing. If you have been successful in the management of your health issues, you have something to offer others. You can encourage others to follow their doctor's orders and take the appropriately prescribed medication, not to mention just being a friend to them in their time of need. The doctor is the expert in medical diagnosis and treatment, but he cannot give you the time that a volunteer can.

Another form of volunteering that we do not hear much about is the giving of one's time to help a small business that may be stagnant in growth or else it is growing very rapidly and becoming a larger company. The latter situation requires another series of management skills—skills you can make known to the management. The volunteer will bring to the table his or her management experiences and share with the company's owner. With your input, the management may realize a need for a standard operating procedure, an employees' handbook, a benefits package document, or rules relative to vacations and sick leave, for example. And just think—the volunteer is not being compensated. Wow! This person—the volunteer—must be "nuts!" No, he or she is not "nuts," but is getting great satisfaction in volunteering in order to help. In helping the small business owner, you are helping us all, for I believe that it is the small businesses that are the backbone of our economy.

There are many more volunteer actions being performed every day of which we are unaware. I believe volunteers receive such heart-felt satisfaction that they often benefit from their activities almost as much as the people they are helping. So let's all remember and say thanks to those wonderful volunteers, especially our seniors, and take notice of their work and how pleasant and happy they are in performing those volunteer duties.

* * * * *

Historical Tidbit from 1958
Dr. Ethel Percy Andrus, a retired high school principal,
founded AARP (American Association of Retired Persons),
the leading nonprofit, nonpartisan membership organization
for people over age 50 in the United States.

* * * * *

Senior Organizations

Seniors are a diverse group, having many interests, skills, family backgrounds and so forth, but one thing we have in common is our age. We share a common history, having grown up in the '30s, '40s, and '50s. This gives us a special bond even in our diversity. The diversity is shown in the variety of organizations that are available today for seniors. The common bond is evident in those who attend meetings of the organization. These meetings allow us to get together to share our lives—past and present.

Typically, the meetings start with the Pledge of Allegiance to the Flag and a prayer. This in itself speaks volumes about what we believe and the values we hold. As a rule, we have a respect for God and country and these feelings run deep. After the opening, there is time for fellowship, business, charity projects in which to be involved, and announcements (like who is ill and needs a card, etc.). There is often a program of some kind or other entertainment activities. We seniors love to play and play we do, with everything from bingo games to traveling together. Our friendships are all enriched and the opportunities afforded through these organizations help us to focus on others—not just on our friends but on the less fortunate as we reach out to help in time of need.

One particular organization I would like to mention is OAKS, the acronym for "Older Active Kids." On July 2, 2001 I had the privilege of speaking to this wonderful organization, which is made up of a group of mature citizens that welcomed me warmly with smiles on their faces. I have found that this response is common to most senior organizations. This, of course, makes for a delightful experience for me as the speaker, allowing me the opportunity to make some wonderful new friends.

One thing that I have learned from speaking at these different organization meetings is that older adults enjoy talking about the good old days. Whenever I share anecdotes about my past from the platform, people in the audience are stimulated to reflect on their own memories and they are anxious to share them with me. Veterans speak with pride about what branch of service they were in and where they served. Ladies talk about their roles in the community in the past. Another wonderful thing about this organization (and I feel is probably true of most) is that there is always a welcome mat for past members to rejoin after having been away for many years. They just pick up where they left off, rekindling those friendships they have held dear.

Now organizations may not be for everyone but my purpose is to share with you a pleasant experience that I had and to encourage you to investigate what's available in your area. I believe you will receive many benefits from joining such an organization. By being active socially and involved in helping others, you will stay a little younger mentally, you will get your minds off your problems, and you will make a positive contribution to society.

Looking to the Future

The future can be defined as being the time yet to be. Although we enjoy taking a glance at the past and reminiscing about shared experiences, we still need to live in the present and look to the future. We all need to determine what kind of people we are going to be and what kinds of goals we will set for the future. As children, we see a long future ahead of us and we think about what we will be when we grow up. Then, as we grow and eventually graduate from high school, we look at the future in terms of educational and vocational opportunities. For many, decisions about getting married and having a family are next in the life cycle. We need to make decisions about all aspects of everyday living and what kind of future we want for our families. There is planning for the children's education, where we will live, financial matters, involvement in community, etc. In most cases, this stage of life is a long one, but if the Good Lord allows us to live into old age, then we face decisions concerning retirement and our future as mature citizens. As seniors, we need to determine how we will achieve our financial goals, enabling us to have a desirable and comfortable lifestyle. We may be faced with decisions about whether or not our grown children still need some financial support. We need to make decisions concerning health issues and the lifestyle that will be required to keep us in good health. Decisions about church and community involvement are important and will determine how we are going to contribute, with the goal in mind of making our society a better place to live.

* * * * *

Historical Tidbit from 1935
In 1935 Roosevelt proposed his social security measures.
In his annual message he declared that the day
of great private fortunes was ended....
Every citizen must be guaranteed "a proper security,
a reasonable leisure, and a decent living throughout life."

* * * * *

All this decision-making may sound tiring, but I believe that this stage of life we call "the golden years" is a wonderful time of life. You may not agree, but if you stop and think about all of the living you have done, taking the good and the bad, the joys and sorrows, you may realize that in the process you have become a better person and citizen. Now with all of this "knowledge of living," let's look at the future and see how we can share, help, and advise younger people on how to make the road smoother for their own future. We are now the mature consultants on how to live and we can offer "suggestions" as to the best roads to take. Let us not neglect this responsibility we have to leave a legacy for our young people—a legacy of wisdom drawn from life's experiences. We all have goals for the future, but the most important decision we need to make is whether or not we are at peace with God, with ourselves, and with others. Let us look to the future with thankfulness for the blessings of the past and a determination to be a blessing to others now and in the future.

Mentoring

A wonderful way to pass on one's wisdom is to serve as a mentor. The dictionary definition of a mentor is "a wise and trusted guide and advisor." How does one earn the title of mentor? The answer is by living life and having experience in the area of interest for the one being mentored.

Let us think for a moment about how mentors have played a role in our lives. As a child I had many mentors. My grandmother was my mentor as it related to being a Christian. She not only preached the Gospel to me but also was a mentor by example.

My grandfather was my mentor as it related to developing a work ethic. His mentoring was more demanding, as evidenced by questions like, "Did you cut the wood and fill the wood box?" However, he set an example by being a hard worker himself and a person of his word. As I remember, I never questioned his direction, for he earned the right to be a mentor. I hope that you will take a few minutes to remember people in your childhood who served as mentors.

Another of my mentors was my football coach, who taught me the value of teamwork. and personal sacrifice. The good running backs were taught to respect their linemen and blockers. You may have experienced teamwork by being in a school play, working on the school paper or working on an assignment in a study group. In these cases, the teacher served as your mentor. In discussions with fellow seniors, it is not unusual for individuals to talk about teachers who had mentored them. What a compliment it is to the teaching profession!

Several years ago I re-entered the work force due to a universal market demand for a specific set of skills that I possessed. The demand for people with this set of skills was so great that the marketplace could not provide the trained personnel. This required the corporations to hire personnel with technical knowledge who could be further trained in other specialties. This is an example of mentoring in the workplace. Whether you are just starting on your career path or are an established professional, there are times when unbiased advice from a seasoned professional can help guide you toward your goals. Mentors provide support, counsel, friendship and guidance. I have found that I benefit as well, as I have associated with a number of brilliant young people. Another benefit is the sense of satisfaction that comes to me as I follow in the footsteps of my mentors, whether in the professional world or members of my family and acquaintances.

From a business point of view, we have now progressed to the point where corporations have planned mentoring programs for a diversified work force. A mentoring program helps workers in the development of their careers. Transfer of training (job intelligence) reduces turnover, which is expensive to any company. Mentors are recognized as "people developers." The career path of the inexperienced person can lead to management positions. Another important benefit for business is that it increases productivity, as well as job satisfaction for the individual workers. The only negative thing that I encountered while serving as a mentor was having a conflict with the person's supervisor, but for the most part, a mentor should be able to avoid this kind of conflict.

I feel that we seniors, having had a lifetime of experience, are qualified to be mentors to the younger members of our family or friends. We need to be alert to opportunities to influence and educate the young and inexperienced. Now we must be "cool" in this process, as I am sure some of the younger folks might wonder what we could know about a particular problem. Well, we do know, and by being good listeners and putting ourselves in their place for specific situations, we can offer alternative solutions to whatever problems they face. What a joy to be a part of this process! I thank God for our mentors, for without them, I know I could not have accomplished so many things that I have done in my life.

Seniors in the Work Force

While it is true that many seniors do have leisure time, enabling them to participate in organizations and volunteer their skills in different arenas, it is also true that many are unable to retire or find that for financial reasons, they must return to the work force after retiring. During recent times there has been an economic downturn in this country and, for different reasons, many retirement funds have gone into the "water trough." This is especially true in instances where retirement funds have been invested in the Stock Market. We cannot know what the future brings concerning investments. We frequently hear the experts making their predictions, but it seems to me that there are so many factors that impact our supply and demand economy that it is difficult to know for sure what will happen from day to day.

It is my view that some companies feel that when you reach your late forties and early fifties that you are professionally "old." When you reach your sixties you are an "antique," and when you are in your seventies you are a "dinosaur," figuratively speaking. Based on the assumption that you are physically and mentally capable to satisfy the position requirements, age should not be a deterrent.

Why? First, let me give you my definition of what I consider to be an "expert." The expert is one who has experienced failure, as related to employment, and has learned from his mistakes. These types of employees have a large contribution to make in our economy—creating a profit for companies and their stockholders.

Now if a company has a need to hire either a part-time or full-time employee that can immediately be productive, why not hire one of these already qualified people? When they come aboard, they will immediately be productive. When you hire a less experienced person, there is a learning curve, depending on the position. This learning curve can take anywhere from three to six months to train the employees. The company must decide if they need someone who can immediately be productive or if they can wait until a person is fully trained. In some cases, the company hires a senior on a part-time basis in order to not only perform the job function but serve as the trainee's mentor. This approach has been utilized in companies that are in the technology business and probably works the same way in other types of business and manufacturing.

Now one might say that companies do not want to incur the expense of a salary to which the senior was accustomed. Well, it has been my experience that the senior who needs the job to supplement his income due to inadequate retirement funds is more than willing to come back into the work force at a lower pay scale. For the senior who just wants to continue to be a part of the work force, the pay is not as much of an issue.

Another thing that seniors bring to the marketplace is their strong work ethic, learned in the days when this was true of most of our nation's citizens. They were taught that if they had to stay late to do a job, they automatically did it, or if they were told to do something that was not in their job description, they did it anyway. This work ethic carries over into the mentoring that they do on the job now. The company can count on them to show up everyday, ready to work. Additionally, climbing the corporate ladder is not one of their objectives. Some have already been at the top and are now content in a lower position. They realize that this will allow them to work without the former pressures that came from being in charge.

So, if you are in a hiring position and need someone to fill a job requirement, I recommend that you hire one of those "old," "antique," or even "dinosaur" individuals who may apply for the job. Look past the gray hair and wrinkled faces to the real treasures that they are, realizing they have much to offer and your company will be better off by hiring them.

* * * * *

Historical Tidbit from 1975
A microcomputer, the first of its type,
which is designed for home use,
is now widely available for sale in the US for $297.
It has 256 bytes of memory and is assembled from a kit.

* * * * *

Seniors and Technology

I had the pleasure some months ago of speaking to an organization called C.O.R.C.C., which stands for County Older Residents Computer Club and what an eye opener it was for yours truly. My speech was on the "History of Technology" and, I must confess, I thought being in the technology business for some fifty years, that I would just "shine with techie knowledge," but I had quite a surprise. What a happy and pleasant surprise on how advanced and knowledgeable these members were relative to personal computers and how proud I was of my senior brothers and sisters. Now to put everything into its proper perspective, I delivered my speech regarding the history of large-scale computers that are the support of industry and government. However, the personal computer is now an essential tool for workers in today's world—supporting their day-to-day activities such as communications and project planning.

Additionally, the personal computer is quickly becoming the predominant communications vehicle for families, students and seniors. I have heard the sayings that, "you are too old to learn" or "you can't teach an old dog new tricks." Well, I am here to say that there is a group of seniors who prove these dogmas wrong. Seniors are learning "new tricks." There are many organizations like the C.O.R.C.C. out there. I suggest that you attend one of these meetings and listen to the programs and side bar conversations before and after the meeting. You will see how sophisticated these seniors are and you might learn something too.

There is even a newsletter called the *Hotline* published for seniors that gives "Today's Tip" and many other worthy news items. To give you an idea of the level of expertise, here is a question from the tip sheet:

Q. I try to use ScanDisk and it never finishes.
A. ScanDisk is a DOS program....

These seniors are learning the language and becoming very savvy about computers.

Now for the reader that has been intimidated by the personal computer, don't be. In fact, when personal computers first came out and were to be used by the major corporation for which I worked, I was given the task of indoctrinating designated people within the divisions to learn how the PC could be utilized in their day-to-day work. So I established an information center and had a very knowledgeable person assigned to teach these people. However, the executives of this large corporation needed this knowledge also, so they received private tutorials. It is my belief that some of them were intimidated by the advent of this new breed of technology called the personal computer, which was understandable. So, for any of you seniors who might want to venture into the age of technology, don't be intimidated, as there are thousands of seniors who use the computers today. We have thrown away the quills in the distant past and now, to some degree, the pencil and even the typewriter are becoming obsolete in the push to use this high-tech tool we call the personal computer.

We should all applaud those seniors who continue to pursue new and exciting ways of doing things and have the desire to continue to learn, for this kind of attitude keeps your mind alert and healthy.

* * * * *

Historical Tidbit from 1995
A global publicity campaign launched Windows 95,
the new computer operating system from Microsoft.

* * * * *

Needless to say, but I will say it anyway—seniors today have many opportunities to grow and learn, participating fully in society. We have a well-established position in our country—one of experience and wisdom—and we should take advantage of these opportunities in order to influence the younger generation that comes behind us. Demographics tell us that we are now the largest population group and we have many organizations and representatives in government speaking up for our cause. So, let us be encouraged to be bold in teaching the young the high standard of societal values that we enjoyed in the past. This is the responsibility for seniors now.

1990-1999
"The Dot.com Decade"

The world seemed to be a safer place as the nineties decade began. Repressive hardline communism collapsed in 1990 in Eastern Europe, and the racially divisive apartheid system was dismantled in South Africa. The Soviet Union and the US declared that the Cold War between them was over.

The newfound peace was short-lived, however, as conflict arose between Iraq and Kuwait, old hatreds between ethnic groups intensified in Yugoslavia and Bosnia, and international terrorists preyed upon innocent citizens around the world. These conflicts involved the United States more and more as our military took on the role of international "peacekeeper."

The turmoil was not confined to remote places of the earth but was very evident in our own nation as well. In the nineties we watched in horror as misguided "terrorists" bombed the Federal Building in Oklahoma City in 1995 and the Olympics Games in Atlanta in 1996. The terror made its way into our nation's schools also as children and teenagers became cold-blooded murderers. Some of our "heroes" fell from their lofty pedestals, and others of them died. One fallen hero was the former football star O.J. Simpson, on trial for murder in 1995. Bill Clinton, President of the United States, was impeached after lying about adulterous affairs. Princess Diana of Wales died in a terrible crash, and Mother Teresa, beloved nun in India, died after a long lifetime of Christian service.

The good news was the Stock Market rose to new heights as America enjoyed unprecedented long-term economic growth. Because of the fall of communism in Europe, more free trade opened up between countries, giving American workers more opportunities. Unemployment was at an all-time low and inflation practically nonexistent. The entertainment industry brought us a surge of all-female singing groups such as the *Spice Girls* and computerized animation in films like *Toy Story*.

The use of computer technology was not limited to the entertainment industry. The nineties were the dot.com decade, ushering us into the World Wide Web. For many, it has been a somewhat scary journey into this world, for there are "terrorists" even on the Internet. Computers became more affordable than ever so there are far more just everyday people who own and operate them. This availability has given rise to e-commerce and e-mail. Computers are here to stay, and the computer business is providing jobs for many. Some of us are even finding ways to use the Internet as a positive force in society, as this communication tool opens doors to the world.

The door to the 21st century has opened to us and we must decide how to bring the wisdom of the past into the present so our future will be secure and our great country will be a great place to live for many generations to come.

SECTION 7

RANDOM REMEMBRANCES

* * * * *

You're not old unless you can recall when...(Source Unknown)
You were sent to the drugstore to test vacuum tubes for the TV.
Kool-Aid and Ovaltine were the only drinks for kids other than milk.
There were only two brands of boys' sneakers.
Nobody but farmers and cowboys ever wore jeans.
It took five minutes for the TV to warm up and there was nothing but
a test pattern on late at night.
A dime was a decent allowance, and a quarter a huge bonus.
At the shoe store you could stand up to a big x-ray and look into
the viewer at the bones inside your foot.
Girls didn't date, wear lipstick, or kiss until late high school, if then.
They never smoked or drank liquor until college, if then.
Your mom wore nylons that came in pairs.
All your teachers wore either neckties or dresses and oxfords,
and the female teachers had their hair done every day.
Laundry detergent had free glasses, dishes,
or towels hidden inside the box.
No family in our town had more than one phone, car, or TV set.
Any parent could discipline any kid, or feed him,
or use him to carry groceries,
and nobody, not even the kid, thought a thing of it.
They threatened to keep kids back a grade if they failed—and did!

* * * * *

CHAPTER TWENTY-SIX

Random Thoughts of Thinking Back When

I find that as I get older there are times when I am alone, maybe
in the front room or out in the yard enjoying the sight of flowers, birds and natural beauties given to us by the Almighty. At times
like these, I find myself reminiscing over my life, reflecting on both
the positive and negative experiences I have had on my journey. I
tend to dismiss any bad memories, however, as I do not want to
revisit those experiences at this stage of my life. Thankfully, I am
blessed that there were not that many to even think about.

Bullies

Many times thoughts come back to when I was a child growing
up and I remember playing "kick the tin can" or "hide and go seek."
I remember the kid who was the bully in the neighborhood that I
tried to avoid as much as possible. Otherwise, he would beat me up.
Finally, I got tired of running and stood up to the bully, even though
I knew I would get a "lickin'." It was worth it, knowing that he
would never bother me again. I'm sure most of us have had similar

experiences. By the way, the weapon of choice was fists, not guns or knives. Now I do not necessarily consider this a bad memory, but just acknowledge that it was just a part of growing up. I had no thought of suing anybody!

Imagine That!

I know that all of you at some time in your life have gone out in the park or out in an open field and have lain down on your back so you could look up to the sky and observe the beautiful white billowing clouds. Or at nighttime, when the sky was so clear and the stars were shining so brightly, you shared with your friend or friends what you wanted to be when you grew up. The imaginations ran wild and no one made fun of your dreams. It was clean and refreshing, those moments of dreaming, and to this day they are still so vivid in my mind. What a memory!

How about going to the movies and watching your heroes on the screen? You would think, "I want to do that" or "I want to be like that person" or "I wish I could sing like that." These are not unique to any one person, in my opinion, but I bet most of us have had those thoughts—another great way to dream. I venture to say that the entrepreneurs of our great country were and still are people who would be classified as dreamers.

* * * * *

Historical Quip from 1943
Heartthrob Frank Sinatra launches solo career.
It's said he drives the girls wild.

* * * * *

Remember those days when there were movies like the "Wolf Man" or "Frankenstein?" On a summer's night, when the movie was over, you would be walking home and there was a mild wind that ruffled the branches of the trees. Your mind started racing as you imagined the Wolf Man was in the bushes, but you kept your head straight even though your heart was pounding and you were saying to your feet, "Get me home as fast as you can."

I guess because we are seniors, our minds have been put on "cruise control," which enables us to have these random thought moments (which is preferable to so-called "senior moments"). It is not uncommon to draw on these past memories when with a younger family member who may be in a similar situation to what we experienced, such as wanting to grow up fast. Our responses will often be "Don't wish your youth away" or "Enjoy the moment, as you will grow up fast enough." In this way, we can get more mileage out of those memories and maybe help someone else along the way.

How's that?

In the past there were words and phrases that had so many different meanings as compared to today. Now I want to share with you some sayings from the past as presented by "Burma Shave." Burma Shave, in order to advertise their products, used road signs that appeared alongside the highway. As we drove by, the kids in the car would make a game of reading them. This was in the 1950s. Remember, in those days, the road was a 2 –lane highway with a low speed limit, so the rider could actually read the very small signs. The signs had clever sayings, and I think that the subtle messages on those signs still hold true today. They were truly enjoyable to read. I viewed these signs on the roadside while traveling on highway 66.

DROVE TOO LONG
DRIVER SNOOZING
WHAT HAPPENED NEXT
IS NOT AMUSING
Burma Shave

THE MIDNIGHT RIDE
OF PAUL FOR BEER
LED TO A WARMER

HEMISPHERE
Burma Shave

Another delight of years gone by that I truly miss is the obvious respect for others' property. We had few cases of vandalism where rebellious youth would mar the looks of buildings with unwanted and profane signs. Today we have graffiti all over the place. The most we did when it came to graffiti was drawing with chalk on the sidewalk for the game of hopscotch. You know, when I think about it, that is not seen so much today. I guess that kids are looking at television or playing computer games.

I remember an incident of a billboard outrage many years ago. There was a billboard atop one of the buildings by the Fox theater in my town. The ad displayed was by a very well known milk company. It pictured a mother holding her baby in her left arm feeding her a bottle of milk from this prestigious milk company. This was fine but there was one thing missing. The mother did not have a wedding ring on her finger. This was not the intent of the company but just an unintentional error. The public noted this error and the company immediately corrected it. Now just think about what you have just read. Ask yourself if this would be an outrage today. Would anyone care?

Music or Noise?

Now I know that each generation has its type of music. The exception to this, as I see it, is classical music that has survived through many generations. But the non-classical music is the type that I am addressing. My generation had Bing Crosby, Dean Martin, Frank Sinatra, Dinah Shore, Kate Smith, Dorothy Danbridge, Ella Fitzgerald, Nat King Cole and the list goes on and on. Throughout those generations that enjoyed this music, and even into the 1950s Rock 'n Roll era, the one common thread was that we could understand the lyrics (words). In today's music, as a rule, I cannot understand the words. In those cases in which I do hear and understand, I find that some songs contain vulgar words, unpatriotic messages, hatred against our law enforcement officers, and the like. While driving, I sometimes hear booming noises coming from the car pulled up beside me (even from several lanes over!). At first I think it is maybe a sonic boom from one of the military jets flying overhead, but then I come to find out it is a car radio blaring from a car somewhere in the vicinity. Sometimes I feel like we are having an earth tremor. Interesting that they call their players "boom boxes!" I don't know how they are able to interpret the language of that music, not only from the vagueness of the words, but because of the deafening noise. I would also imagine that we have an increase in hearing problems in the generation that is now growing up.

Disappearing Act

The current atmosphere in this country not only tolerates this expression of free speech in any and every manner, but it has caused so many words to lose their meaning—words like character, respect, values, morality, integrity and godliness.

These words have not completely disappeared from our language yet but the day may come when we relegate the concepts they embody to the museums of history. There are numerous things that have nearly or completely disappeared from our culture from the days when we rode the streetcar to work or did laundry in a wash tub and hung it on the line to dry.

Just Plain Ole' Neighborliness

Many things I don't necessarily miss, but one thing I do miss is the personal interaction with neighbors and those who served us. It's not that people are no longer friendly or that we don't get to chat with the store clerk occasionally, but there is such a rush-rush atmosphere in our society, it is easy to get the feeling that no one has time for leisurely conversation or helping one another.

Remember how it used to be in neighborhoods? The neighborhood family has disappeared for the most part. In earlier days, all the neighbors knew each other and talked to one another. People did not come home and lock themselves into their houses and re-appear in the morning. I remember the frequency of block parties, which also seem to have disappeared. I remember the wives getting together in the morning and having coffee and a roll prior to getting to their household chores. Now my wife and I, in our mature years, have been blessed with having some wonderful neighbors, such as Alan, Chris, Bob, Wanda and Ted. Having them as neighbors gives us a flashback to the good old days when family-oriented neighborhoods were the norm. We took pleasure in seeing Alan come home and hollering, "How you doing, young man?" Or seeing Wanda and hollering "How you doing?" Or seeing Bob in the yard having a nice conversation or seeing Ted and asking how his business was going. The point is that they were interested in us and our family and work and we in turn were interested in them. What a beautiful neighborhood family we had!

What are some other things that have disappeared? How about places like the local shoe repair shop? In our town, the shop was owned by Tony and it was over Goldie's Department Store. As our children got older, we took their shoes to Tony. In addition to having our shoes repaired and shined, we had good conversation. Every customer was on a first name basis, and we were always asked about how our family was doing. Tony's shop is long gone but every once in a while I think about having my shoes repaired. Nowadays when our shoes are worn out or in need of repair, we throw them away and buy new ones. Also, we now wear those light running shoes, as they are more comfortable. It's funny how foot fashion comes in cycles—white socks have made a comeback and are now an "in thing." I remember that in addition to getting the shoes repaired, we could also get all-leather items repaired, from belts to ladies' purses. There are a few such shops still in existence but you really have to search them out. I miss Tony and his shop but time marches on, and so must I, so I will now put on my Nikes and start marching.

Another source of great conversation was the local barbershop. Just recently I lost one of my barbers, who was not only an excellent professional, but was a great person. I did not see him socially but, when he cut my hair, we had great conversations. He was a very nice man. Now I still go to my favorite barbershop, as his partner is also a great barber and a great person and we have great conversations. But the main thing is these barbers cut hair the old-fashioned way. To me the old time barbershop is slowly disappearing.

As mentioned before, I really miss the old time gas stations, when you drove in and they filled your gas tank, cleaned your windows, and checked the air in your tires and finally the oil. Nowadays you drive into most stations and you fill your own gas tank, clean the windows, check your own oil and try and find the air compressor to fill your tires. Then you walk into the station and give them the pump number so you can pay. While you are in there you can even buy your groceries for the week—just a little humor.

The old-time service stations were, for the most, part full service stations, in that in addition to the basic service, they also did mechanic work. Today we have specialists, with shops such as one for tire service, one for mufflers, one for transmissions, and some to just sell you the parts for you to install yourself. Ah, for the days of true customer service!

* * * * *

How to Know You're Growing Older

Everything hurts and what doesn't hurt, doesn't work.
The gleam in your eyes is from the sun hitting your bifocals.
You feel like the night before, and you haven't been anywhere.
Your little black book contains only names ending in M.D.
You get winded playing chess.
Your children begin to look middle-aged.
You finally reach the top of the ladder,
and find it leaning against the wrong wall.
You join a health club and don't go.
You begin to outlive enthusiasm.
You decide to procrastinate but then never get around to it.
Your mind makes contracts your body can't meet.
You know all the answers, but nobody asks the questions.
You look forward to a dull evening.
You walk with your head held high trying to get used to your bifocals.
Your favorite part of the newspaper is "25 years ago today."
You turn out the light for economic reasons rather than romantic ones.
You sit in a rocking chair and can't get it going.
Your knees buckle and your belt won't.
You're 27 around the neck, 42 around the waist,
and 106 around the golf course.
Your stop looking forward to your next birthday.
After painting the town red, you have to take a long rest
before applying a second coat.
Dialing long distance wears you out.
You're startled the first time you are addressed as "old timer."
You remember today, that yesterday was your wedding anniversary.
You just can't stand people who are intolerant!
The best part of your day is over when your alarm clock goes off.
You burn the midnight oil after 9:00 p.m.
You back goes out more than you do.
Your pacemaker makes the garage door go up when you watch a pretty girl go by.

The little gray-haired lady you help across the street is your wife.

You get your exercise acting as a pallbearer for your friends who exercised.

You have too much room in the house and not enough in the medicine cabinet.

You sink your teeth into a steak and they stay there.

(Source Unknown)

* * * * *

Conclusion

"Legacy – a gift of personal property by will." When we think of legacy, we think of what we might inherit. Depending on the orientation of the heir, one might think, "How much will he leave me in his will?" We do tend to think of material goods, stocks and bonds, property holdings, etc. From the viewpoint of one who is nearing the end of his earthly life, he or she will give great consideration to what is handed down to the next generation. Even if we are not near death, it is not out of the ordinary for those of us who consider ourselves senior citizens to begin to think of what we might pass down to our children and grandchildren. There will be the usual things like house and property or monetary wealth. Also, there probably are some special things included in your list like a favorite brooch handed down to you by a grandmother or a special pocket watch that belonged to your grandfather—true heirlooms, regardless of monetary value. They are special because of who they come from and are to be treasured by the recipients.

These material things are wonderful and desirable, and sometimes even needed, gifts. However, just for a moment, I would like for us to think of legacy in a different way. Have you thought about what other kinds of gifts you may have to pass down? If you have lived an honorable life, you pass on the gift of integrity. If you have endured through much trial and self-sacrifice, then you pass on the gift of perseverance. For me, I know I inherited a strong work ethic from my grandfather and a love for the Bible from my grandmother. How can you put a price on that kind of inheritance? Perhaps you have been a teacher and have passed on the gift of knowledge to your students and a love for knowledge to your own children. Or you may have been in the medical field and have demonstrated great concern and care for those who are suffering. Perhaps you have been "just a mother," but your years of staying home with the children have paid off in terms of offering your children a stable home life. In this shaky world in which we live, that is saying a lot, and I think God probably has special rewards for this kind of mother.

Character, integrity, a strong work ethic, faithfulness, good citizenship, good sportsmanship, a good sense of humor, a love for music, joy, faith—these are all part of the legacy we can leave for those who follow us. I have tried in this book to stimulate your thinking, causing you to remember those events and those people that helped make you who you are. It is my hope and desire that, as you reflect on these things, you will realize that you have quite a valuable inheritance to leave your children. You must tell them the things you have learned from life. They will know about the values you hold dear, for you have lived these before them, but don't miss the opportunity to relate to them the stories from your past. The time you share in telling the stories will be precious to your loved ones after you are gone. Be willing to invest yourselves in people and you will be rewarded richly.

I hope you have enjoyed our walk down "Memory Lane." This walk has taken us into the past momentarily, but we must not dwell there. We must seize the opportunities in the present that God gives us to influence our world and then look to the future with hope and faith.

Notes

Chapter One

1 Quotation attributed to John Paul II [Karol Wojtyla] (b. 1920), Polish ecclesiastic, pope. Quoted in Observer [London, Dec. 7, 1986]. From *The Columbia World of Quotations*. New York: Columbia University press, 1996. www.bartleby.com/66/.

Chapter Three

2 *Encyclopedia Brittanica,* Student Edition, 2003 CD/ROM, s.v. population.

Chapter Six

3 *Encyclopedia Brittanica,* Student Edition, 2003 CD/ROM, s.v. education.
4 *Encyclopedia Brittanica,* Student Edition, 2003 CD/ROM, s.v. automobile industry.

Chapter Nine

5 *Encyclopedia Brittanica*, Student Edition, 2003 CD/ROM, s.v. Sherman, William Tecumseh.
6 Source for quote unknown.
7 Source for quote unknown.
8 Bartlett, John, *Familiar Quotations 10ᵗʰ Edition* (Boston: Little, Brown, and company, 1919), xix, 1454 p. 23 cm.

Chapter Eleven

[9] *Encyclopedia Brittanica,* Student Edition, 2003 CD/ROM, s.v. Thanksgiving.

Chapter Twenty

[10] *Encyclopedia Brittanica,* Student Edition, 2003 CD/ROM, s.v. Christmas

Endnotes

1 Quotation attributed to John Paul II [Karol Wojtyla] (b. 1920), Polish ecclesiastic, pope. Quoted in Observer [London, Dec. 7, 1986]. From *The Columbia World of Quotations*. New York: Columbia University press, 1996. www.bartleby.com/66/.

2 *Encyclopedia Brittanica,* Student Edition, 2003 CD/ROM, s.v. population.

3 *Encyclopedia Brittanica,* Student Edition, 2003 CD/ROM, s.v. education.

4 *Encyclopedia Brittanica,* Student Edition, 2003 CD/ROM, s.v. automobile industry.

5 *Encyclopedia Brittanica*, Student Edition, 2003 CD/ROM, s.v. Sherman, William Tecumseh.

6 Source for quote unknown.

7 Source for quote unknown.

8 Bartlett, John, *Familiar Quotations 10th Edition* (Boston: Little, Brown, and company, 1919), xix, 1454 p. 23 cm.

9 *Encyclopedia Brittanica,* Student Edition, 2003 CD/ROM, s.v. Thanksgiving.

10 *Encyclopedia Brittanica,* Student Edition, 2003 CD/ROM, s.v. Christmas.

Printed in the United States
25531LVS00004B/73-105